# ZEN
## AND THE ART OF
# DOG TRAINING

# ZEN
## AND THE ART OF
# DOG TRAINING

### What Dogs Can Teach Us
### About Ourselves

## ADAM HALLECK

PURE INK PRESS

PURE INK PRESS

Paperback ISBN: 979-8-9875866-4-8
Epub ISBN: 979-8-9927468-2-2

Library of Congress Control Number: 2025915879

www.pureinkpress.com

*For Lala, my greatest teacher, my guardian angel, my best friend. I feel blessed to share this grand adventure together.*

# Contents

## CHAPTER 1

# The Beginning

On that cold November morning, the sky was clear, but the roads of the winding Pacific Coast Highway were slick from a downpour the night before. Traveling with my girlfriend from our home in Santa Rosa to Sea Ranch, California—a small, rural community located several hours north of San Francisco, our route took us along the teetering cliffside, perched over the ocean's abyss.

We planned to hike through the forests and hunt for any type of prized edible mushroom. My life was about to undergo a drastic change.

The thick canopy of redwoods kept the coastal forest floor dank and humid, a perfect condition for mushrooms and all sorts of other wildlife to grow. Our trip that day uncovered more than we bargained for.

After a few hours of trudging through the brush, climbing under bushes, and picking any mushrooms we could find, we decided to head home. We sorted through our findings, discarding anything inedible or not in prime condition. Though our payout was slim, the true reward was spending a day in nature.

Shortly after we began our drive back down south, I came to an abrupt stop.

Two stray dogs were wandering across the highway. Initially, I wanted to let them pass and continue on home. However, when I saw them continuing to meander and sniff about, oblivious to the dangers of a fast-approaching vehicle, I pulled over and herded them off the road.

Of the two dogs, one seemed very friendly and came up to us willingly, while the other was quite wary of us and required coaxing. The first was a small, stocky, forty-pound Shar-Pei mix with a black coat and a blue tongue. The hair around his muzzle was graying, and he had a slight glaze over his eyes. He came over, hopped right into the car, and immediately accepted our affection. Comfortable around humans, the dog appeared to have had an owner at some point. The other dog, a mixed breed with striking Shepherd features but a sleek, short coat, kept her distance. She was skinny; her tail was low but not tucked, and her ears were poised and alert, pointed with the black tips flopping over. Each time we took a step toward her, she would recoil, jumping back several feet, only to creep with curiosity toward us again. While she was less fond of people, she was considering following suit now that her packmate was in our car.

Luckily, there was a general store called Stewart's Point right across the street, so I ran over and explained the situation, asking for dog treats or anything that might help. They sympathetically offered me a handful of salami.

I grew up terrified of dogs.

As a young child, a large Labrador mix lunged at me and latched onto my shoulder, biting me and leaving me with multiple puncture wounds, deep bruises, and emotional trauma. At around age twelve, while I was skateboarding at a friend's house, a large Pit Bull escaped from his neighbor's fence and charged at us. Using my skateboard as a shield, I pushed the dog away, and we quickly climbed the nearest fence. Luckily, I got out with only a small scratch on my leg, but the experience triggered my earlier trauma. While I never disliked dogs, I hesitated to approach any unfamiliar dogs due to my experiences. For a while, I was even quite timid around our family's dog, Blaze, a large

2

and neurotic German Shorthaired Pointer. As I grew older and taller, my fear of dogs developed into a healthy respect and caution.

On the highway that day, with 22-year-old me and my girlfriend coaxing the younger dog, I realized that I wasn't the only one apprehensive about our meeting. Although she did not seem trusting, I sensed a desperation and submissiveness that put my anxieties at ease.

After about thirty minutes, I thought of creating a trail of salami leading to the car, which she thankfully followed. I then gently lifted her into the backseat. Once the pup was in my car, I could get close enough to notice how dirty and emaciated she was. Both dogs were covered in ticks, fleas, tree sap, and scars. They must have been traveling for days, if not much longer. As she crawled from the seat down to the floorboard and curled up, I could see her trembling from stress and exhaustion.

With both dogs in the car, I decided to head to the nearest town with a veterinary clinic.

Our first stop was Gualala, CA, just north of Sea Ranch. Upon arrival, the vet welcomed us in, provided us with slip-lead leashes, and scanned for microchips, but neither dog had any chips or identification. They checked the dogs for major health concerns and examined their teeth for their ages. The older dog was between twelve and fourteen years old, while the younger was between nine and twelve months old. She said the dogs were probably part of a wild pack that steals food from a nearby Native American reservation several miles east of Gualala and had probably wandered off. Many dogs in those parts were strays. The vet urged us to take the dogs to the Humane Society down in Sebastopol, close to where we lived, because if they ended up in the overcrowded shelters that far north, they likely wouldn't have much of a chance of getting adopted or surviving.

We loaded the dogs back into the car and continued the long journey south.

The anxiety of the new environment, coupled with the sway of the winding road, didn't make for a smooth ride. Although the older dog had no qualms about the movement, the puppy had likely never experienced being in a car before that day. She was less tolerant of the turbulence and proceeded to vomit every ten minutes, which stretched our trip from an hour and a half into a three-hour endeavor, filled with stops, towels, and foul smells.

A lifetime later, we finally arrived at the Humane Society in Sebastopol just before they closed, only to discover they had no vacancies. As it was already late in the evening, they asked us to take the dogs home for the weekend and go to Santa Rosa's Humane Society when it opened on Monday. With nowhere else to go, we had no other choice but to do so. I truly wanted to help these dogs, but I couldn't shake my discomfort. I did not want either of us to become too attached to the dogs and was eager to be free of the responsibility.

We lived in a cramped three-bedroom house with another couple, an old friend of mine, and my buddy who stayed on the couch. When we arrived home, we let the dogs run around in the backyard with everyone. The puppy, whom I had named Gualala (Lala for short) after the town where we found her, finally started opening up. She pranced around our small yard as if it were heaven, and the caution she had expressed seemed to dissipate. She freely came up to each of us, tongue hanging out of her mouth with what appeared to be a joyful smile on her face. It was as though I could feel the gratitude spilling out of her as she let us pet her and playfully dance around with her. Although still a little timid, she was truly relaxing and beginning to learn to trust us.

Everyone lost themselves in the elation of the moment, but I couldn't fully immerse myself in the revelries. My logical brain knew that, being in my early twenties, I was not in a good financial position to take care of any life other than my own. I naively felt that I had the trajectory of my life figured out at that time, and a dog required far too much time and effort. I detached myself and tried to remain somewhat emotionally distant. I didn't feel ready.

Luckily, the universe had other plans for me.

The next morning, I woke up early and took the dogs to a self-serve dog wash where I gave both of them a deep clean bath. The older dog seemed to love it and easily let me scrub, rinse, and dry him off with the blow dryer. The younger pup gave me a much harder time. I wrestled her into the bath, leashed her up, and began rinsing her down. I cleaned her ears, cut tree sap out of her fur, picked off a dozen ticks, shampooed her, and rinsed her again. Although I could tell she wasn't too happy about the whole experience, I sensed that she was grateful to be taken care of. I bought her a leash, collar, and crate, took both pups home, and got ready for work.

While I was bathing them, my girlfriend received a call from the Gualala Veterinary Hospital saying that they had found the owner of the dogs, who would drive down later that day to pick them up. I went off to my job as a busboy at a local bistro, relieved that the situation would be over by the time I got back.

When I returned home that evening, the older dog was gone as expected, but Lala greeted me at the door. Apparently, there was a miscommunication. The person who called claimed the older dog but said they had never seen the younger.

So, there I was, face-to-face with the dog that would change my life forever.

Lala's tongue was hanging out, and her tail was wagging as she looked directly at me. In her deep, brown eyes, I saw the same desire to be loved and accepted that I felt so deeply within me. It was as if those eyes were telling me she was finally home, and all my emotional resistance to the idea of keeping her was futile. Reluctantly, I decided that we would let Lala stay for a week to see how she acclimated to the home. During that first week, she never went potty in the house, didn't destroy anything, and was overall pretty well-behaved.

One week turned into several, and as I bonded with Lala more and more, I also found myself having constant anxiety and occasional panic attacks. I did not take the new responsibility lightly. I was young and felt as though I could barely take care of myself, let alone another being entirely dependent on me. To quell my anxiety, I began walking, exercising, and training her every day. We would go on morning bike rides for miles to deal with her excessive energy. At lunchtime, we would go on training walks. I had no idea what I was doing, but I had a collar, a leash, and a pocket full of treats.

Every day, we would take the same walk, and I would teach her commands such as sit, down, stay, and heel, all to relative reliability. Within a few months, I could walk Lala off-leash through our neighborhood. It wasn't even close to bulletproof, but we were seemingly getting somewhere.

Although Lala was making progress responding to commands while walking through the neighborhood, she began exhibiting behavioral issues that I couldn't understand. She had extreme reactivity toward people, particularly men with hats and beards, although it could be anyone within twenty feet of us. She would lunge and bark and would only stop if I forcibly removed her from the situation. It didn't help that I constantly had her off-leash, which meant that I had to run after her to ensure she didn't attack any random stranger she considered a threat.

She would even exhibit this behavior with people she knew. Soon, regardless of how much my roommates and friends loved her, they got fed up with her behavior. Whenever we all met up at the skate park or volleyball court, I'd bring her and tie her up. She would inevitably ruin everyone's experience because she simply would not chill out. She was constantly on edge and barked at anyone within eyesight. I stubbornly would not leave her at home and continued bringing her everywhere in the hopes that through exposure, she might improve.

Her antics were sometimes stressful, but rarely bothered me.

What affected me was that I was the only one she showed her true self to. With everyone else, aside from a select few, she was closed off and wary. Even my grandfather told me I should get rid of her when he met her. Never was I discouraged; I was intent on getting through to her so she didn't have to feel so fearful and stressed all the time. I didn't know it then, but my dedication and doggedness would be the exact qualities needed to make an excellent dog trainer.

Within a few months of training, I had grown accustomed to people chastising me for irresponsibly letting my dog off-leash, but it never swayed me. I continued to train with her regularly when I was not at work. One day, I was walking Lala and training her in a nearby park when a man yelled, "Hey!" from across the street. Anticipating conflict, my thoughts began cycling through witty comebacks and remarks to handle what I assumed would be yet another person harassing me about keeping my dog on leash. I looked up, irritated, to see a large man smoking a cigarette outside his home, a neighbor I would often pass by, but had not spoken to before.

When I met his gaze, he yelled from across the street, "Do you do that for a living?"

He caught me off guard. I had no idea what he meant. At the time, professional dog training was unknown in that community.

"Do what?" I asked, after a moment of discombobulation.

"Train dogs," he said.

"Oh, no, this is just my dog," I replied as Lala's dopey grin beamed up at me.

"Oh, well, you should. You're good at it." He went back to smoking his cigarette casually.

All my defensiveness melted away in confusion, and it dawned on me that he was complimenting me. I hastily called, "Thank you!" and returned to training my pup.

That was the first time I ever considered becoming a dog trainer or even realized that being a dog trainer could be a career. I didn't know what that meant or how to go about it, but the thought piqued my curiosity. That man's compliment planted the seed. I look back on that moment as a pivotal point in the trajectory of my life.

A year later, I moved to Los Angeles to pursue a career as a professional dog trainer.

Becoming conscious of the give-and-take dynamic with Lala was not easy, nor was it intentional; it happened organically over time. It took deep suffering for me to see how my relationship with my dog was simply a reflection of my relationship with myself.

While still in Santa Rosa, I went through a difficult breakup that left me emotionally in shambles and led me to move back in with my mom.

On a seemingly normal day, I got a call from my girlfriend. She had been on vacation while I watched Lala at the house. In tears, she told me we were breaking up, which completely took me by surprise. I wasn't even aware that anything was wrong with our relationship.

I did not take it well.

I took Lala and left the house we had built a life in together. Everything I thought I had been building for nearly five years came crashing down, and it was all totally out of my control. Depression consumed me. I tried setting boundaries and giving myself space to grieve, but I had a difficult time accepting the separation. She later regretted her actions and continued trying to contact me, even showing up unannounced at my mom's house or the skate park to try to reconcile. While I felt tormented, still a small part of me yearned to return to the familiarity of our relationship.

After months of this back-and-forth and internal conflict, I was an emotional wreck and realized something needed to change. I decided to try to cut ties once and for all and went to retrieve the last of my things that I had left behind at the house. I was hoping for some closure and thought maybe one final conversation with my former girlfriend would allow me to feel at peace. When I arrived, I saw a new but familiar robe hanging where my robe once hung. Seeing the home we had made together being inhabited by someone else broke me, as if our nearly five-year relationship meant nothing to her. During that grueling conversation that I'm not proud of, I learned that even before we broke up, she had been seeing a friend of mine. After I left, he moved in. Her disclosure of infidelity crumbled the last of my remaining dignity.

Although I felt betrayed, deep down I was still attached to the life we had created together. I didn't know how to let go, how to move on, how to recover from this one final blow to my ego. I felt my entire identity shatter. With nowhere else to turn, I had to face my demons: the foundational illusory projections, expectations, and beliefs upon which I had "built my life." I didn't want someone else's choices to define my story. A small part of me bravely took responsibility for the emotional mess that was my life.

I wasn't aware of it then, but when my heart broke, shattering my entire identity, the pain from losing the relationship was only the tip of this emotional iceberg. When I was a child, my parents divorced, shifting my whole reality; the stability I once felt evaporated. My mother left my father to do some soul-searching, and he fell into a deep depression for years. Unlike my two brothers, I felt deeply aware of the pain that existed in the home. Although daily life continued in a seemingly normal way, a dark cloud constantly loomed overhead, filling my life and strongly affecting me, even though no one talked about it. I took on much of my father's pain but couldn't understand why I was so sad and anxious all the time. Because my life on paper was good, I never allowed myself to truly feel these emotions that were altogether too overwhelming for a child to comprehend. It continued to be too much for me to handle, and at a young age, I began rejecting my family, feeling as though I didn't fit in or belong.

As my brothers excelled in school, my social and scholastic life suffered. I stopped joining family outings and began skateboarding and smoking weed as ways to escape the bleak emptiness of my existence at home. Switching back and forth between my mother's house and my father's house allowed me to remain emotionally detached from everyone. Even though I deeply craved stability, I looked for any excuse I could find to go off on my own. During that time, skateboarding was the only thing that brought me a sense of joy and freedom. Years later, after trying to create the emotional stability I craved, the feelings of betrayal, heartbreak, and unworthiness from my breakup triggered the emotions I had been suppressing.

I was emotionally unstable, raw, and fragile, but I remembered how it felt to be a child, skateboarding around without a care in the world. I yearned for that sense of freedom and wondered if I would ever feel it again. Luckily, at the suggestion of my father, I began therapy. It turned out that my therapist had previously been a Buddhist monk. He sent me down a rabbit hole of literature on self-growth, meditation, and Buddhism. My days became filled with reading, meditation, and spending time in nature with Lala. Working with Lala became the highlight of everyday life. No matter how despondent I felt, she always showed me the path to presence and joy.

So what does meditation have to do with dog training?

I remember my first moment of true self-reflection during dog training. Back then, although Lala gave me a certain level of obedience, the reliability was minimal, which brought anxiety and frustration into the training sessions. While at my mom's house, I began training behind the church across the street. One day, while walking home with Lala, I noticed that my tongue was throbbing, which startled me. I realized I had been biting it out of frustration for almost the entire training session. Then I noticed how tense my body was and how fast I was breathing.

Up until then, I had not developed self-awareness as a skill, but realizing that I was that aggravated while doing what I loved most in the world—spending time with my dog—was confusing. I didn't then have the context or emotional intelligence that I do now, almost ten years later, so I wasn't able to understand what it meant or what I could do about it. Eventually, this desire to grasp the mind-body connection, along with a recommendation from my therapist, led me to meditation, which trains the mind. Soon, meditation became part of my daily routine along with training Lala.

Lala became one of my most significant sources of healing and self-exploration.

Once I brought the spiritual dimension into dog training after moving to Los Angeles, I truly started to appreciate what I was creating. I wasn't building a foundation of training or obedience, looking for a particular set of behaviors, or trying to teach my dog a bunch of useless party tricks. I was forming a deep connection with Lala, and, as importantly, a connection with myself. For the first time, I was able to see my habitual behaviors and thought patterns. I began to figure out who I was outside the confines of an ego that protected me from seeing the undesirable traits beneath my surface. This ego tried to control every aspect of my experience. Meditation inspired an inner journey that led to the most meaningful shift in how I related to my dog and the world around me.

My dog became my most profound spiritual teacher.

## CHAPTER 2

# Relationship

Training a dog, no matter what tools or techniques we use, is all about intentionally building a very specific relationship: one that has clear boundaries and roles to ensure it is healthy and balanced. Creating a more fulfilling life experience with our dogs requires that we clearly understand the roles we play and how to meet our dogs' needs. Most dog owners approach training without a clear idea of what they want or how to achieve it, much less the role they play in their relationship with their dogs. Without forming a bond, the dogs will likely develop behavioral issues, neurotic mental states, and become emotionally unstable. When we establish clear roles in our pack—the pack could be as small as you and your dog, or as large as you and the entire house full of family members or roommates, including any other potential pets—and learn to meet our dogs' needs effectively, we can live a more harmonious and satisfying life together.

## Meeting Our Dog's Needs

In a truly healthy and balanced relationship, it is our job to meet all of our dog's physical, mental, and emotional needs. As the human, that is the role we play. We should understand these needs distinctively, although they often overlap.

A dog's *physical needs* consist of food, water, shelter, and exercise. A dog whose physical needs are not met will become unhealthy from malnourishment, dehydration, or obesity. Physical needs are perhaps our dogs' most obvious ones to fulfill, and most dog owners I encounter are sufficiently taking care of their dogs' physical needs.

Our dogs also have *mental needs*. They require stimulation that allows them to consistently engage their minds in problem-solving and develop intellect and understanding. These results involve setting clear boundaries, maintaining clear communication with our dogs, and giving them a sense of responsibility within the pack. I tell my clients that if you don't give your dog problems to solve, they will give you problems to solve. If you don't give their mind something to do, they will take out that pent-up energy on something else, which is where behavioral issues begin to develop. It is common to see mentally under-stimulated dogs looking for mental engagement elsewhere, such as fixating on prey during walks or becoming reactive to other dogs around them. The simplest way to understand this behavior is to recognize that your dog needs a job to do. By showing them clearly how to use their intelligence to serve their pack functionally, it helps create stability and balance for the dog. These mental needs are often met to a minimal extent by the average dog owner, but rarely are they entirely fulfilled.

Lastly, our dogs have *emotional needs,* which are the most subtle and vary from dog to dog. They consist of a combination of exercise, socialization, affection, freedom, playtime, and structure; we can allocate these elements in varying degrees to meet the drive of the dog in front of us. Meeting a dog's emotional needs requires that we provide our dogs with adequate outlets to use their energy in a functional manner. But without meeting their emotional needs in conjunction with their mental needs, there is a high chance the dog will become emotionally unstable and develop dysfunctional and potentially harmful behavioral habits. Many of the most common behavioral issues, such as reactivity, separation anxiety, and aggression, are symptoms of emotional instability. It is our responsibility to teach our dogs how to use this energy, or drive, to serve the pack in a manner that aligns with our lifestyle.

In training, the obedience commands—sit, down, and stay—serve as a language to begin working with the dog emotionally. By working with commands with varying levels of distraction, we can guide our dogs to perform under stress. Over time, we can gradually increase the levels of stress and distraction to prepare the dog to fulfill their role in everyday life. It means that while teaching our dogs simple commands, we also build their ability to carry out these exercises in various circumstances we might find ourselves in. When done appropriately, the dog builds emotional resilience, and we deepen the strength of our communication with them.

## Being the Leader

Meeting a dog's needs requires us to lead the pack.

By reserving the right to make final authoritative decisions for our dogs, we can better set them up for success in day-to-day activities. Typically, we will make better decisions for our dogs than they can for themselves in our chaotic modern environment. We better understand when to cross the street, what may be a threat, how to earn food and shelter, and how to behave to conform to society's expectations functionally and appropriately.

As a dog trainer, I teach dog owners how to fill the role that their dog needs.

Oftentimes, this approach to training forces people to behave in ways that don't feel natural to who they *think* they are. I work with feminine women who need to learn artful masculinity to meet their dogs' needs. I urge men who are typically rigid and disciplined to be more emotional and flexible to meet their dogs' needs. I work with individuals who lack confidence, helping them discover their inner strength, and those unaware of their arrogance, guiding them to learn caution. In Buddhism, this collection of conditioned behavioral patterns and beliefs of "who we think we are" is referred to as the *ego*. Often, it is this ego that stands in the way of the relationship we want with our dogs and the one we actually have.

Although I rarely say it bluntly, in dog training, I aim to bring awareness to the person's ego and where it may be inhibiting their growth and the process of bonding with their dog. Meditation and mindfulness are methods of breaking our ego's constant influence on our thoughts and behavior.

Taking a passive role in building this relationship will have negative consequences.

Obvious and tragic examples are a dog getting hit by a car if they are off-leash or out of control, needing surgery if they ate something dangerous, or being injured from getting in a fight with another dog. On the other hand, these consequences can be as subtle as a dog being left out of daily activities if they cannot behave appropriately.

If our dogs are too reactive outside, pull too much on the leash, or won't reliably comply with our commands, they will end up getting left at home more often than not. Often, the dog's poor behaviors result in a life resigned to the home with only a walk or two to break up the monotony. If their behaviors are too burdensome, we will not include them when attending weekend road trips, family events, our kids' soccer games, or running errands around town.

When we fail to lead adequately, our dogs suffer, and we suffer.

Two years before finding Lala, I experienced firsthand what repercussions can occur when a dog's needs are unmet. My best friend had adopted a Husky puppy on a whim and named him Loki. All of us who lived in that house worked restaurant jobs and were unavailable most of the day. I remember the day he bought the puppy—he brought it home, dropped it off with me, and went off to work. At that point, I had no idea how to meet the puppy's needs. My friend's approach to caring for the dog involved no training or structure, because he believed Loki was intelligent and didn't need guidance to figure out the world. Loki quickly became a confident and aloof Husky that didn't listen to anyone. After several months of the dog peeing in the house, escaping to run in the neighborhood, and eating just about every sock he could find, we had to ask our friend to move out with the dog.

He and Loki moved back to his parents' house on three fenced-in acres not far away. To us, it seemed to be an ideal place for a Husky. On paper, it was perfect, but the problem was that even with all that room to run, there was little to no structure or engagement with this intelligent, high-drive dog. The pup, then a year old, was left in the yard most of the day. He began exercising his prey drive and constantly brought dead animals back to the house. It started with small animals such as rats and squirrels, but eventually he started bringing home rabbits, raccoons, skunks, and even a cat. That went on until one day he escaped the eight-foot fence and ended up attacking and mauling the neighbor's goats, all of which died. After two years of distress, my friend reluctantly decided to rehome the Husky, understanding that he was not meeting the dog's needs. Although the dog was rambunctious and sometimes downright frustrating, we were all fond of him, so it was heartbreaking to see Loki be rehomed. But without getting the engagement and structure that he needed, Loki devolved into his animalistic instinct and never learned how to behave appropriately.

By guiding our dogs effectively, giving them functional outlets for their drive, and setting realistic boundaries, we can provide them with the most fulfilling life possible. When we train our dogs, we give their minds and emotional energy a task that is in alignment with our lifestyle. We teach them boundaries so they can have a realistic expectation of how the world around them works and, more importantly, how they fit into it, which gives the dog the best opportunity to live a harmonious life in a home.

As responsible dog owners, that is our job.

Training is about building a relationship in which we have an understanding with our dogs on a deep emotional level that they can trust our guidance more than their instinctual response to stimuli—that our decisions will get the best possible result in any given situation. This relationship will offer any dog and its owner a higher quality of life, because from here we can effectively meet all of their physical, mental, and emotional needs. Leader, alpha, CEO, top dog, *kahu*, guardian, head honcho, emotional-support-human—you can call it whatever you want. When we, as dog owners, play this role in the pack and lead with deep compassion and an unwavering dedication to serve our dogs, everybody wins.

CHAPTER 3

---

# Pack Structure

To best serve our pack, we need to understand how dogs socially organize and approach their universe. All dogs are instinctually dominant, no matter their size, breed, or temperament. Therefore, if we don't lead effectively, they will take it upon themselves to begin making authoritative decisions for the pack. When we don't effectively guide them through life, showing them exactly how to behave in all the environments we find ourselves in, they will rely upon their instincts to determine how to respond to the stimuli around them. Because their instincts did not evolve to exist in our modern lives harmoniously, dogs often develop dysfunctional behavioral responses, such as pulling on the leash, jumping on people, becoming reactive toward other dogs or various triggers, guarding food or objects, barking excessively, or chasing birds and squirrels.

Leading effectively is essential to building a balanced relationship.

Without proper communication and leadership, there is a disconnect between our experience and our dogs' experience: Our dogs may feel that they are serving the pack, but to us, their behavior can feel incredibly frustrating and dysfunctional. These behavioral tendencies, when left unchecked, become habits for our dogs, which can jeopardize their safety, health, and overall well-being in the wrong environment.

## Social Hierarchies

For more insight into how we may fit into our dogs' lives and how they fit into ours, we should first look at how dogs organize themselves socially. Dogs, similar to wolves, are pack animals, not unlike ourselves. In observing wolves' behaviors, we can see how the pack structure operates. Less clear might be how we fit into this structure.

Dogs descend from wolves; in fact, many breeds share 99.9% of their DNA with wolves.[1] Although wolves in their natural environments organize based on breeding, wolves in unnatural environments, such as our homes or sanctuaries, organize in packs with a hierarchical social structure, based on size and temperament, in which one member assumes a dominant position. In a video describing the social structure of wolves, Dr. L. David Mech, a biologist specializing in the study of wolves, tells us that "in an artificial pack, when you put many wolves in different assemblages together—unrelated wolves… would form a… dominance hierarchy."[2]

We can observe this behavior at any dog park as the dogs begin to establish a hierarchy. The more dogs there are, or with multiple dogs that have dominant temperaments, the more complicated this hierarchy becomes. The pack member with the most dominant temperament keeps balance in the pack and dictates the subordinate relationships. This role holds the most significant responsibility in the pack. Given your knowledge and understanding of how to thrive in your environment, it follows that you are best suited to lead the pack.

## Communicating Leadership

When dogs are puppies, the mother gives feedback based on the puppies' behaviors and decision-making. It's not uncommon for mother dogs to grab pups by the nape of the neck to move them around or to discipline them, showing them where they can and cannot be and how to behave appropriately. Pack members further up the hierarchy will also growl at, nip, or pin down the puppies to set certain boundaries. This original structure for dogs is natural and is how they learn manners and social etiquette. Once they enter our homes, we often struggle to provide adequate structure or teach appropriate behavior and pack etiquette, particularly since the rules governing our world are more complex and nuanced. As their caretakers, it is our job to pick up where their mother left off and begin providing this feedback consistently to ensure they learn to traverse their environment appropriately. This principle is relevant to puppies and to any dog we invite into our homes. As soon as a dog enters a new environment with new social dynamics, it learns either that there are rules and boundaries to follow or that there are no rules or boundaries. It is up to us to communicate our expectations and reinforce them until they become standardized behavior from the dog.

What is our role in this whole dynamic?

To keep our dogs safe and to give them the highest quality of life, we must train our dogs adequately and develop a relationship in which we hold the leadership position and the responsibility that comes with it. We prove ourselves to be formidable leaders day in and day out by consistently and fairly communicating boundaries and dictating as many aspects of our dogs' experiences as possible, all while maintaining an excellent standard of living for them. When we lead effectively and consistently meet our dogs' needs over time, we earn their trust on a much deeper level. We demonstrate that we provide safety and the necessities of food and shelter, and also that we can meet their emotional and mental needs, as discussed.

Once this relationship is firmly in place, unconditional trust follows.

With clear direction, dogs begin to fall into place exactly where we need them, trusting that every decision we make for them—using the language of obedience training—is in their best interests. With so many dangers around every corner, such as cars, chicken bones, and coyotes, we will manage this terrain better while keeping the pack safe and happy. With consistent and focused effort, we can create unconditional trust that transcends all distractions and circumstances, making training reliable no matter where we take our dogs.

Intentionally structuring the pack hierarchy with us at the top gives a greater quality of life and a deeper connection for us with our dogs.

Currently, I have five personal dogs: Lala, Funcik, Yogi, Peanut, and Pachouli. When they socialize freely in the yard or at the park, it is immediately apparent that there is a hierarchy. Lala is the oldest and most dominant. Her stability influences the rest of my ragtag gang of misfits. She will dictate the energy of the pack when anyone gets too rowdy. Funcik, the Pug, falls next in line. Next is Pachouli, the French Bulldog, who will occasionally challenge Funcik's position in the pack by trying to bully her out of her bone. This action has, unfortunately, resulted in some dramatic fights between them, which we've had to forcefully break up. I have a few scars on my hand from these encounters. Now that Pachouli has been with us for longer, the hierarchy is more established, and these fights are much less frequent. Peanut, my Pomeranian and next in line in the pecking order, generally gets along with the rest of the pack, but prefers antagonistically wrestling with Funcik and bullying his older brother, Yogi. Yogi is my Belgian Malinois and is the biggest dog in my pack, weighing in at sixty-five pounds. He is also my most submissive and softest, falling at the bottom of the hierarchy. When we are all together in public, people often ask me who the alpha is in my pack. My answer is always a resounding "me."

When we understand the social organization of dogs and how we fit in, it becomes obvious what relationship will create the most stability for everyone in the pack. Since humans understand the modern environment where we live better than dogs, we will make decisions that result in greater well-being for all. These attributes make us excellent candidates to lead our dogs effectively.

## CHAPTER 4

# The Pendulum

The amount of disciplined structure and spontaneous leniency at any given moment dictates the *balance* in our emotional relationship with our dogs. From here, we can expand or contract the dog's autonomy to meet their immediate emotional needs. Similar to the swing of a pendulum, the relationship between the human and the canine within dog training is never static. The balance in the relationship is a constantly moving target that we travel toward, but it is not a destination, nor is it a thought or concept. True balance can be experienced as a feeling of equilibrium, which we can learn to recognize and tune into while spending time with our dogs. Looking closely, we can see that their behavior results from how much balance is present in each moment.

Our dogs' behavior can signal which direction our pendulum is currently swinging. By understanding and consciously taking action to establish this balance, we can begin to truly know our dogs. If they behave poorly today, it is often due to a lack of consistency in our communication and guidance in the past. *Imbalance* occurs when we feel out of touch with our dogs or experience discord in the relationship. During these periods, there will be a feeling of unease and tension between us and our dogs, usually felt as frustration or anxiety, although it can take other forms as well. A breakdown in communication and a general disrespect for the roles in the relationship indicate periods of imbalance.

Our dogs are constantly aware of this relationship and will act based on their trust in our guidance, which is determined by our level of consistency in our behavior. If our dogs are behaving well or being obedient, it is an indication that we are fair and consistent in how we guide them. Boundaries and roles in the relationship are established and respected. During these periods, there is a certain feeling of peace and equanimity between us.

This is balance—when relations in the pack are clear and stable.

Regardless of the level of training, every relationship will fluctuate between these two poles to some extent. It is up to us as humans to be aware of this fluctuation and work to keep the pendulum stable. We could ease up and allow some spontaneity if we have been very disciplined, or tighten up the structure and routine if we have been too lenient or lacked presence. Depending on our level of awareness in the relationship, these pendulum swings can last minutes, hours, days, or even months.

## Harmony and Discord

Misbehavior is generally a sign that we have allowed too much freedom for our dogs, whether intentionally or not. This occurrence doesn't have to be frustrating or defeating, but it can be an obvious indication to tighten up our structure by asking more from our dogs throughout the day. Going through moments of imbalance is not indicative of an unhealthy relationship. As dog owners, we should allow our dogs certain freedoms as they prove themselves reliable. Although these freedoms are necessary, they affect how much *influence* we have over our dogs. Influence refers to how much our words, energy, body language, tone of voice, and presence shape our dogs' behaviors and decision-making. By bringing an acute awareness to where our pendulum is, we begin to notice imbalance sooner, on increasingly subtle planes, and can respond appropriately to move the relationship back toward balance.

During periods of sustained balance, we feel a harmony between us and our dogs. We notice less pushback in our structure and guidance. There is a sense of ease in handling our dogs, a lack of tension in the body. The dogs are not as easily swayed by distractions, fears, and the temptations of the outside world. We feel more comfortable and confident, which allows us to bring them to more places. These are periods when trust is at its height, creating some of the most fulfilling moments, when our investment of hard work pays the dividends of an enjoyable harmony in the relationship. With the right effort, awareness, and understanding, we can gain momentum, and our influence will dramatically increase, thus achieving a deeper sense of balance for more extended periods.

## Mastering the Pendulum Swing

How do we master the pendulum swing of the relationship with our dogs?

It begins with self-discipline and mindfulness of our influence over our dogs in each moment. When in true balance with our dogs, our influence supersedes any surrounding distractions.

Small distractions expose the root of the issue as a lack of influence over our dogs and a fragile relationship. These moments can be helpful if we know how to find insight within the experience. They point us in the direction of where our relationship could use the most work. It is up to us to maintain an awareness of the balance and create a relationship that can weather unpredictable storms of daily life.

Instead of puppy-proofing the world, we are world-proofing the puppy.

With influence, we can show our dogs how to respond to the stresses of life appropriately. We trust in our dogs to follow our guidance, and they trust us to guide. An example would be a dog following a relaxed heel on a busy street, effortlessly ignoring another dog across the street that is lunging and barking. These intervals of ease can last days or months without any destabilizing incidents. In this relationship, we must have the authority to expand or contract the dog's experience of their environment as necessary to meet the needs of the situation. A dog needs certain behaviors and boundaries to exist functionally and safely in a public park. That same dog needs an entirely different set of behaviors and boundaries to exist functionally and safely in a restaurant or airport.

Understanding our dogs, ourselves, our pendulum of balance, our surroundings, and how to navigate these elements with grace is the key to mastering our relationship.

As humans, our pendulum of expansion and contraction in our daily lives is the constant fluctuation of emotion. Sometimes, life can feel spacious, joyous, and free. Other times, it can feel dark, heavy, and claustrophobic. We cannot always, if ever, control these feelings or the thoughts or circumstances that cause them. Still, with practice, we can condition ourselves to be less reactive to the outer situations of our lives and maintain a balanced mental and emotional state.

It is not the thoughts, feelings, or events that determine our suffering; rather, it is our acceptance or rejection of the present moment, exactly as it is. By resisting the present moment, we suffer. Alleviating our suffering is less about changing the external conditions around us and more about becoming familiar with our emotional landscape. We can develop the same acute awareness of our emotions and thoughts, feeling them in their fullness, and accepting them without impulsively reacting or identifying with them.

Our external circumstances and experiences, due to their unstable nature, will always be unreliable sources of happiness. While explaining the ancient eastern philosophy of Taoism in his book *The Meaning of Happiness*, Alan Watts says, "The secret of this harmony... is not action but acceptance... We do not alter the actual situation; but our attitude toward it undergoes a change whereby we feel harmony where before we felt discord."[3] Always looking to things outside of ourselves for fulfillment leaves us without agency and out of balance. Because we have little influence over these environmental factors, looking for stability in our ever-changing surroundings is futile and will only lead to disappointment and suffering.

## Resistance and Acceptance

Instead of trying to chisel our lives to fit into our narrow set of preferences—our likes and dislikes, fears and desires, cravings and aversions—we can choose to accept things as they are and appreciate what the experience may have to offer, regardless of whether it is desirable or not. Oftentimes, it is our most difficult moments that catalyze the most transformational growth. The situational circumstances of our lives can never bring lasting happiness or joy. What determines our overall emotional state is our habitual, mental reaction to these circumstances, or our thoughts and feelings about it, and the level to which we accept our present moment experience.

Do we emotionally resist that which we cannot control? Without awareness, we fail to see that it is our *resistance* to reality that causes our suffering, rather than our surroundings themselves. From this perspective, we are victims of our opinions and feelings about the outer circumstances of our lives. By observing and accepting our experience as a part of life, of being a human on this planet floating through infinite space, we can find a sense of wholeness and a clear vantage point that embraces our joy, pain, boredom, pleasure, fear, and the entirety of our emotional spectrum.

Meditation is a practice of seeing things as they are without resisting them.

With practice and consistency, we can begin to differentiate between a situation and our emotional reaction to it. We can see the situation as it is and understand our thoughts *about* it. As we sit with our thoughts, we can observe our repetitive mental reactions to our emotions. We tend to cling to and grasp pleasure and resist or fear pain. It takes brutal self-honesty and an uncompromising self-compassion to transform one's conditioned structural mental blueprint. Dissecting our value system to its core creates space, allowing us to influence our behaviors and actions instead of continually indulging in our impulsive reactions to our thoughts and emotions. In breaking down and reconstructing our perceptions, we transform the world around us and, in turn, transform ourselves.

When I began meditating, it was not easy. Sitting with my ruminations of pain and betrayal made minutes feel like centuries. At first, it seemed almost unbearable to accept and breathe through the emotional turmoil I was experiencing constantly. I felt completely lost as my identity crumbled. Anger, despair, and worthlessness consumed me. I began to see the self-serving qualities of my deceptive mind with all the ulterior motives and transactional natures of each of my relationships. For years, my mind had used a sort of logic to deny emotional vulnerability, and in meditation, the floodgates were opening.

Finding peace and acceptance did not happen overnight. Although I had glimpses of peace initially, it took faith in the process and myself over months before I saw any shift in my way of thinking and feeling. Further, sadness and pain still colored the moments of contentment that I encountered. But there seemed to be a space around it. I was learning to sit with my emotional experience without resisting it. The resistance—the unwillingness to feel—and the mind's frantic efforts to shield me from pain kept it cycling through me again and again. Once I began to let it run its course, allowing my experience to be without trying to control it, peace arose naturally. By ceasing to constantly *do* something about how I was feeling, I was able to let go and accept life as it was.

To find balance in our pendulums, we look to not-doing. That doesn't mean we do nothing. We still respond to the needs of those around us, except we find stillness within ourselves before acting. This stillness allows us to respond appropriately with a greater sense of awareness of the whole. Instead of reacting based on our conditioned, habitual responses, we can have a deeper and broader perspective, creating emotional space between us and the situation itself. From this place, we can act in alignment with the issue, as conscious participants and not victims.

Meditation is the practice of not-doing.

In today's modern world, our constant *doing* consumes us so much that we forget how peaceful it is to simply *exist*. So many responsibilities fill our days to get by: taking out the trash, driving to work, doing dishes, walking our dogs, grocery shopping, or cleaning the house—from the moment we wake up until we go to sleep, there always seems to be something that we have to get done. All this doing constantly presents the mind with problems to solve—one after another. Without creating space in our lives between all this activity, physical or mental, we forget how to sit and simply be present. The mind becomes conditioned by the experiences we have and, even more so, our feelings and thoughts about these experiences.

Alan Watts touched on this when he said, "A person who thinks all the time has nothing to think about except thoughts. So, he loses touch with reality and lives in a world of illusion."[4] Meditation allows us time to breathe between the constant flow of stimuli that we experience every day. From here, we can begin to see beyond the illusion. It is the practice of allowing the proverbial dust to settle so we can look at the world with a fresh perspective.

If we can begin to see our lives without our mental projections, acknowledging our perceptions as illusions, we can see how our misperceptions are generally the cause of our suffering. Again, this process must happen organically by naturally allowing our minds to settle without artificially constructing new illusions of how meditation *should* look or feel. We must get out of our own way. The natural transformation will occur as long as we surrender to the idea that there is *nothing* we can do to *cause* it to happen, just as we cannot force a flower to bloom, nor can we force a butterfly from its cocoon. By setting aside time to meditate and follow our breath with a sense of curiosity and openness, we experience the transformation of how we see the world.

## Resilience and Inner Stability

Our consciousness begins to transform when we develop awareness of our pendulum.

We can then become aware of expansion, the feeling of spaciousness and relaxation, and contraction, the claustrophobic feeling of tension and darkness, in our lives. By becoming aware of our internal experiences, we can navigate the course of our personal growth. Without the development of this awareness, we risk being reduced to biochemical organisms, perpetually reacting to the stimulus of the environment, victims of our emotional swings and the uncontrollable circumstances in which we find ourselves. By developing this consciousness, we can find a middle path between the highs and lows of our circumstances, therefore finding the foundational peace and stability beneath our fluctuating emotions.

Whether we look at how we relate to our dogs or ourselves, we can see the swing of a pendulum striving toward balance. A balanced relationship has a strong element of emotional resilience. When working with our dogs, it is essential to take calculated action and initiative during training to find this harmony. We can expand or contract the extent of freedom or structure to navigate the emotional landscape of training. By taking calculated action, we can cultivate emotionally resilient dogs capable of handling the fluctuating situations and stresses of life around them.

Developing healthy habits and practices will allow us to maintain awareness of balance, establishing inner strength and emotional resilience to respond more appropriately to the needs of those around us, including our dogs.

## CHAPTER 5

# Finding Freedom in Structure

Sometimes, the idea of training our dogs can seem daunting. We may feel as though we don't have the time or energy, or we don't know where to begin or how to progress—we can feel paralyzed by the sheer perceived magnitude of the task. However, training our dogs doesn't have to be work all day, every day. Instead, we can shift our perspective and learn how to incorporate basic training into our lives so it doesn't feel as if it's work at all. By creating structure for our dogs and introducing boundaries, we strengthen their trust in our decision-making and build healthy habits.

A dog's life should always have some amount of structure.

Structure is the core that allows us to maintain our relationship with our dogs. Without structure, we are left without any standardized modality of life, making it a challenge to condition appropriate behavior or recondition inappropriate behavior. Implementing structure means consciously setting boundaries to dictate the behavior and activities of our dogs' everyday lives.

As their trainers, we give them a role, a job, to fulfill within the pack. This job could be as simple as walking calmly next to us in a designated position instead of pulling and sniffing randomly about.

It could be lying down on their bed for extended periods instead of aimlessly wandering around the house without purpose. Using formal commands—sit, down, and stay—helps guide our dogs in the direction of desired behaviors. Instead of allowing them the freedom to indulge in instinctual and potentially neurotic behavior, we show them exactly how to behave appropriately in any given situation.

Structuring their lives shows leadership and sets realistic expectations for acceptable and appropriate behavior.

Simple things that integrate training into our daily lives can make a huge difference in our relationship with our dogs. In other words, we can find ways to *work smarter, not harder*, to achieve the most remarkable depth possible in the relationship and optimize the most functional communication between us.

*Structure* is the implementation of systems, rules, and boundaries that we use to maintain a line of communication with a dog that actively contributes to the growth and depth of the relationship. With so many moving parts in our lives, controlling certain variables becomes necessary in cultivating appropriate behavior in our dogs. The more consistent we can be throughout the day, the more reliable and predictable their behaviors will be. The more aspects of their lives we can influence, the more we will understand the environment in which they function and, therefore, more accurately read their behaviors and respond appropriately.

The heart of all training is building a relationship and a line of communication with which we can influence our dogs' impulsive and instinctive reactions to stimuli and help guide them to more appropriate alternatives. With structure, we can do this without overexerting ourselves along the way.

Since we need to allocate some time and energy to meet our dogs' daily needs, I recommend that my clients work with their dogs in a formal training setting for fifteen minutes, twice per day. This routine is achievable even with the most demanding of lifestyles. (If one isn't able to give their dog at least a few minutes of quality attention every day, maybe they should reassess pet ownership.) These two training sessions constitute roughly two percent of the day. What are we to do for the other twenty-three and a half hours? To maintain an adequate level of consistency, we can apply structure in all aspects of their lives.

Given that many of us have busy schedules and professional training can be quite costly, here is some advice for maximizing the return on your time and energy investment while training your dog. Even if you've trained your dog previously, applying these guidelines will allow you to use the training more functionally in your life. I recommend training your dog to understand these three essential pillars:

1. Crate your dog when unsupervised
2. Reinforce a heel position on walks
3. Practice the down-stay at home

## Three Pillars of Structure

### CRATE TRAINING

Every dog owner I've worked with comes to training with a different perspective. They have their past experiences, expectations, and reservations—and none of their dogs are alike either. It is common for me to meet those who don't believe in crate training. Almost every single time, these reservations came from a lack of understanding of their dogs' needs and how to fulfill them properly.

Part of implementing structure is utilizing the crate functionally. By using the crate when we're gone, and at night when we're asleep, we begin to lead even in our absence. Seeing as it is impossible to be fully present with our dogs for twenty-four hours a day, we must use specific tools and exercises to reinforce our relationship with our dogs consistently. Using the crate properly is an effective way to increase and maintain our influence. Otherwise, by leaving our dogs alone and unattended, even if they don't exhibit destructive behavior, we allow them to put themselves in harm's way and learn to make decisions without our feedback. Every moment our dogs are free to make unchecked decisions is a moment with a negative impact on our training progress.

Furthermore, with proper training, placing the dog in a crate communicates a clear time and location to decompress, which is crucial for their mental and emotional well-being. Many dogs will develop unhealthy neuroses without structured decompression time. The crate allows us to regulate the number of stimuli the dogs experience. A puppy that should be sleeping sixteen to twenty hours per day needs that time out, or they won't get a healthy balance of rest. It's similar to nap time for kids. By limiting the stimulation around our dogs, we give them time to process information from training and rest their bodies and minds as their brain develops.

The crate is never a punishment.

I want the crate to be a safe place for my dog to relax and decompress while I'm gone, asleep, or unable to supervise properly. Dogs, being den animals, enjoy tight, cozy spaces. When we decide that the crate is the safest place for them to be, we should see calm, relaxed behavior in the crate when we ask for it as a clear sign that our dogs trust in our decision-making.

Negative associations with the crate generally stem from gaps in the foundation of communication with the dog or uncertainty around the roles we play in the relationship. A dog that reacts to the crate with distress is uncertain of the motives and outcomes of the decisions we make for them. Placing them in a crate takes away their agency, and a dog who equates their agency—and not our leadership—to their quality of life will experience emotional resistance to the structure of a crate. Building the relationship alongside introducing the crate will give us a higher chance of making our dogs comfortable with relaxing within the safety of the crate.

## HEEL POSITION

The second pillar of our three-point training is teaching a dog to walk in a heel position properly. Many behavior issues that happen on walks, from leash-pulling to aggressive reactivity, could be avoided by teaching a heel position on walks. The heel position refers to the dog's toes aligning with the heel of my left foot as we walk. Although the side is arbitrary, training dogs to walk slightly behind and in a designated position allows us to lead effectively. Keep in mind, this activity is different from loose-leash walking. Even with a loose leash, if we position the dog ahead of us, they are much more likely to exhibit behaviors such as excessive sniffing, pulling, reactivity to other dogs or people, eating off the ground, or any other challenging behaviors. When we fail to create clarity and engage with our dogs sufficiently, they start looking for engagement with things outside the pack. Teaching a heel position will add structure and an added level of communication to produce a better understanding between the human and dog. Especially for nervous or shy dogs, they will feel safe and secure as it becomes the default position. For a rambunctious, confident dog, the heel position will initiate the accountability needed for walks to be free of frustrating pulling or excited lunging. A heel position will build the structure needed to continue developing influence and impulse control on our daily walks and beyond.

## DOWN-STAY

The third pillar I suggest is the down-stay, which I emphasize because of how powerful this simple task can be. Implementing down-stays will allow our dogs to connect with all parts of our lives. Between the training sessions and walks, we can still integrate training, make space for decompression time, and teach impulse control. We can start by practicing at home and eventually bring our dogs with us to more aspects of our lives. I cover the down-stay in more depth in Chapter 6.

My dogs accompany me to work, to stores, to the skate park, to Jiu-Jitsu classes, on vacation, and beyond, all because they can lie down and stay, walk nicely with me, and relax in a crate. Looking deeper, while I value those behaviors, what is most impressive about my dogs is that they are emotionally stable. Introducing structure promotes greater emotional stability. Because my dogs get to come with me safely and appropriately, our quality of life together is exponentially greater. Practice these three pillars of structure to increase your pack's quality of life, experience deeper connection, and just have more fun together.

## Finding Freedom

Another aspect of structure that we often overlook is understanding how and when to give our dogs freedom. In certain circumstances, it can elevate and strengthen the bond with a dog, while at other times, it can be detrimental to the integrity of the relationship. Freedom can be our most valuable resource if given with intention. But if our dogs inherently have freedom all the time, then it is not something we can provide, and thus it loses its value. By limiting autonomy to certain places, times, and activities, freedom becomes a reward we give our dogs, valued as quality time and as part of our overall structure, not separate from it.

At the beginning of the training process, I only give releases after training sessions. This routine teaches the dog that freedom is earned and eventually progresses to off-leash hikes, playtime at the park, or wherever our next adventure leads. The rest of my dog's time is structured, with training, walks, down-stays, or crate time. As we progress in the training process, our dogs can spend more and more time with us in our daily lives as a result of the behaviors we cultivate during training. In giving freedom strategically as a part of our structure, we offer *real* freedom: emotional resilience and adaptability (plus off-leash hikes and adventures!).

Giving our dogs free rein of the house at all times comes at a cost.

When we allow our dogs the ability to make any decision they want at home, whenever they want, we permit complete indulgence in their instinctual drives and desires. They become confident in their ability to make decisions that net favorable results, such as taking the most comfortable spot on the couch, sitting next to the most lenient family member at the dinner table, or barking out the window at the neighbors passing by. When the dog brings this belief outside the home, it results in pulling on the leash toward any other dog, squirrel, or person, barking to get what they want, jumping on people, or even running away from their seemingly irrational fears, such as the garbage truck or a plastic bag in the wind.

Whatever relationship we build inside the home comes with us wherever we go.

If a dog feels that our needs are not a priority inside the home, we can't reasonably expect reliable behavior anywhere else. This relationship will then severely limit their freedom where it matters most: outside. Structure in the home allows us to build a bond with intention and mindfulness, keeping our end goal of *real* freedom in mind.

With structure, we build influence in the home first, then we bring it with us outside. Seeing as it is nearly impossible to keep a watchful eye on your dog at all times, you can rely on the boundaries you set to maintain an influential role in the pack throughout the day. Without upholding these boundaries, the dog will continue to lose privileges until its life is limited to just the home and the yard (if you're lucky enough to have a yard), with maybe a couple of short walks in between.

The longer behavioral issues exist, the more liberties our dogs will lose.

A dog that barks relentlessly, pulls endlessly, steals food, or cannot generally self-regulate emotionally is unlikely to be invited to the next family barbecue, Sunday brunch, or spontaneous weekend adventure. I know many owners who dread walks with their dog because of the frustration of being pulled down the street or reactivity toward other dogs. This experience is not healthy or balanced.

As a trainer, I can never change a dog's temperament. However, through a systematic approach and careful training, I can teach a dog how to adapt its behavior to its immediate environment and be comfortable in states that require more focus and self-control. A dog that roams the house freely at all times may get much more "free" time in total, but the drastically reduced *quality* of their freedom will make them much less emotionally stable. Structuring the home for our dogs means that they won't miss out on the rich and fulfilling experiences that come with a regimented life in training. If we stay one step ahead and set boundaries in the home and daily activities— having them lie down on their beds for certain periods, putting them in a crate when we aren't home, asking for a designated position on walks, allowing supervised freedom for play, and keeping to scheduled meal times and potty breaks—we intentionally create a relationship in which we communicate that our decisions are what afford the dog a quality lifestyle.

Just this structure, in and of itself, is half of training.

Without this portion, we are working harder, not smarter. We are creating mixed signals by trying to lead in some instances, for example, on walks, and being complacent and passive in others, such as when our dogs are alone in the yard or the home unsupervised. The lack of clear pack roles, responsibility, and accountability creates an imbalance in the relationship, which is the cause of most of the anxiety and behavioral issues we see in dogs.

As highly intelligent social beings, dogs thrive with clear communication and an understanding of how they fit into our lives. Although the idea of taking a hands-off approach to owning a dog may appear to make your dog "happier," by taking initiative and building a strong relationship, we set our dogs up for success, meet their social needs, and give them a much more fulfilling existence, leading to more equanimity and less stress for all.

Instead of leaving our dogs to themselves throughout the day, giving them structured tasks and routines to follow engages their minds and helps build a deeper connection between dog and owner.

CHAPTER 6

# Down, Stay

Because dogs' instinctive reactions are predominantly obsolete in modern society, it is up to us to make sure they are acclimated and able to live harmoniously among life's many distractions. The down-stay, which trains our dogs to lie down and stay on command, is one of the most important skills to teach, because once our dogs can reliably hold this relaxed position for extended periods, we can include them in so many more enriching activities. We can bring them to coffee shops, restaurants, friends' houses, the gym, and on an airplane, for a few examples. It also gives them relaxation time and eliminates the majority of behavioral issues that exist in the home. From a down-stay position, our dogs can't chew up the furniture, pee on our new rug, or frantically defend the perimeter of our house or property. Instead of releasing neurotic pent-up energy with purposeless activity, the down-stay allows them to decompress adequately.

The down-stay is less about teaching the mechanics of what the "down" and "stay" commands mean, and more a way to work with our dogs emotionally and train appropriate behavior using impulse control and emotional regulation. It trains them to let go of the instinctual drives that generate all that tension so they can finally relax and restore.

We are teaching them that the world can continue to go on around them, and that they don't need to attend to every little thing that may happen. At first, they will still feel the urge to act on these impulses. Over time, with consistency, and above all, patience, we demonstrate how to maintain unwavering trust in our leadership and newfound calm amid the chaos of our modern backdrop.

## Meditation for Dogs

The down-stay is a form of *meditation* for dogs.

By assuming a relaxed, submissive position, dogs begin to relinquish the need to react to everything in their environment. They learn to tolerate and relax into the world around them. Meditation is the practice of training the mind to stay grounded in the present moment without reacting to each emotional or mental impulse that arises during the sitting. It requires a level of concentration, discipline, and self-control. When we tell a dog to lie down and stay, we are asking them to meditate.

Even though they might smell food or hear the doorbell, they learn to remain in their down position and resist the urge to get up and steal a piece of pizza or bark at the delivery person. Without our input and feedback, dogs develop the belief that their assertive behavior earns them the comforts and security they instinctively seek. With repetition and consistency, our dogs will develop greater impulse control, emotional self-regulation, and confidence in our ability to lead and provide for them.

At this point, you will encounter your dog's stubbornness.

With the down-stay, we intend to build impulse control in the dog over time. When working the down-stay, we start in an environment free of distractions. I begin by placing the dog into a down position, lying them down on their bed or a comfortable, designated area with their leash and collar on. The plan is to bring the dog back to the bed each time they get up. Early on, we stay very close to our dogs, praising calm, relaxed behavior. When they inevitably get restless and wander off, we calmly approach them, grab the leash, guide them back to the bed, place them back into the down position, and tell them to stay.

Repeat these steps as necessary. Begin with periods of 15-30 minutes. End the exercise with a clear release, a command indicating that the formal training session has ended and they are "off duty." (With my pack, I use the word "okay" to release them from all formal commands.)

As the dog begins to relax into it, we can move to longer and longer periods of down-stay. During this process, we will see the dog's willfulness. Nevertheless, no matter how many times they get up during the set time, we will address them and bring them back to their spot. When the dog becomes more comfortable with the structure, we can start going about our day more freely. Try walking to the kitchen and back, going to the restroom, or checking the mail. I encourage my clients in this practice for several hours each day. This consistency cultivates the impulse control dogs need to handle the stresses of life.

We can use the down-stay to slowly desensitize and acclimate our dogs to anything that triggers their fears and insecurities. Once we have mastered this command with them for passive behavior in a calm environment, we can slowly begin to introduce higher levels of commotion. Distractions are an integral part of training because they help bring the skills from the training session into the real world. I used these exact exercises with Lala to help conquer her reactivity.

## Setting Aside Distractions

As a trainer, I always look for distractions while working with my dog to test the reliability of our communication. In Los Angeles, we can find various stimuli around every corner. It could be another dog walking by, a pile of old nachos in the street, the sound of the garbage truck, or a squirrel in a nearby tree. Wherever they come from, I welcome distractions in training because each destabilizing moment is another opportunity to recognize and return to balance.

In situations where my dog encounters high-stress stimulation, I often utilize the down-stay. From this passive position, I communicate to my dog that it is not their responsibility to address every garbage truck that drives by, every dog walking past, or every human in the vicinity. I ask for and reinforce calm, passive behavior to instill functional habits into our day-to-day activities. Every formal training session that involves difficult moments prepares both my dog and me for triggers when we least expect them and communicates what behaviors are appropriate in any given situation.

Through consistent practice, we set our dogs up for success in almost any environment.

Self-control and emotional preparation are beneficial for humans as well. We experience a range of emotions and impulses, such as fear, pain, and anger, so we must learn how to handle our emotional landscape with composure. In his book *A Path with Heart,* Buddhist monk and author Jack Kornfield describes the experience of our minds as similar to the wandering mind of a puppy: It has a hard time keeping still. He says, "Calm yourself by relaxing into the breath. When your breath becomes soft, let your attention become gentle and careful, as soft as the breath itself. Like training a puppy, gently bring yourself back a thousand times. Over weeks and months of this practice you will gradually learn to calm and center yourself using the breath."[5]

When our thoughts and emotions become too overwhelming, we can lose our composure. In our lifetimes, we will experience all manner of circumstances and sensations, many of which will be painful or uncomfortable. Although we cannot avoid these feelings, we can begin to relate to our pain, restlessness, self-doubt, or anxiety with gentle compassion, coming back to the present moment with each breath.

When my five-year relationship ended abruptly, I found myself victim to a constant flood of negative thoughts and emotions. Everything reminded me of the life I felt I had lost, triggering panic attacks and deep depressive bouts. I couldn't drive down the street in my hometown without fear of seeing my ex's car. I realized I had no control over my anxious thoughts or unstable emotional state. Seeking to learn about my mind and emotions—my inner world—I read about and began to practice a Mahayana Buddhist meditation technique, developed by American-born Tibetan Buddhist, Pema Chödrön, designed to confront our pain with compassion.

## Becoming Still and Present

Meditation is the practice of being still and present with oneself.

Begin by sitting in an upright position, your spine straight but relaxed, your legs folded in front of you. Then, follow your breath as you inhale and exhale, to become aware of the sensation of the chest expanding and contracting, as well as the breath at the tip of the nose or lips. Sit in the vast space of the mind, watching it as it meanders through patterns of habitual thought. Bring attention to everything in the present moment, allowing your awareness to gently hold your entire experience: your breath, thoughts, the aches and discomforts of the sitting position, the sounds of your surroundings, your emotional state, or any sensations that arise, like the feeling of a cool breeze or the warmth of the sun.

Inevitably, thoughts will arise and carry us away during the sitting. We don't try to force the thoughts away or resist them. Instead, we welcome them to come, and just as easily let them go. The trick here is not to get caught up in them or give them attention and energy that allows them to sweep us away. Each time we notice ourselves becoming lost in thought, pulled back into the past or projected into the future, we gently bring ourselves back to our breath. During a five-minute sitting, we may be surprised by how ingrained our patterns of thinking are, how often they take over our attention, and how many times we return to the present moment. These thought processes dictate our perceptions of the world, and without seeing these perceptions objectively, it can be challenging to change them. We are unaware of so many factors that condition our minds and behaviors, but by observing our habitual thought patterns, we can become conscious participants in our own conditioning.

With practice, meditation deepens our self-awareness and opens our hearts to all of life.

Meditation practice helps me live more fully by allowing me to be more present in every moment. I see my habitual reactions for what they are: conditioned thought patterns projecting illusions onto the world around me. By seeing these patterns, I am better able to discern the difference between a situation and my *reaction* to the situation. In the space between the event and my reaction to it, I can see more objectively, which allows for a response to arise that is more suitable and compassionate. Instead of reacting impulsively to whatever thought or emotion spontaneously emerges, I can sit with these thoughts and feelings, breathe mindfully, and respond consciously and appropriately. I am not perfect every time, and I still experience unwholesome thoughts and emotions. I am human, but step by step, I find that I am slowly getting to know myself much more profoundly and choosing to show up with greater awareness, honesty, and compassion for myself and others.

Developing compassionate and appropriate responses is an essential aspect of effectively leading our dogs.

Maintaining a regular practice helps me to develop the skills necessary to bring this newfound mindfulness and awareness from my meditation into daily life. Without practicing in a structured environment, it can be difficult to identify and change my impulsive reactions, especially when I am suffering. Working with minor difficulties during my daily meditation helps build the capabilities I need to appropriately handle the inevitable heartbreak and loss that takes place throughout life.

Meditation allows us to become nonreactive to the impulsive urges that tend to get us into trouble.

Another emphasis in meditation is the stillness of the sitting posture. By sitting truly still, we can begin to watch our impulses as they arise, inhabit our bodies and minds, and eventually fall away. Zen priest Peter Coyote describes this stillness in his book *Zen in the Vernacular* when he says, "If you've ever meditated, you've observed how difficult it is to do something as simple as sit still and pay attention to your own posture... We're training our intention and housebreaking our personalities as if they were puppies." When we are completely still, not indulging even the slightest urges to scratch an itch or adjust our posture, we can observe the mind and its tendency to grasp. Even when our gaze wanders, it can detract from the depth of the sitting. Can we sit with an urge, like an itch, no matter how uncomfortable, or do we react without even noticing? Coyote goes on to say, "Disciplining the body is a direct way to discipline extraneous mental impulses."[6]

The same goes for our dogs. Meditation benefits them as much as it benefits us. Barking relentlessly at the delivery person will not only get your dog into trouble, but it can also cause dramatic emotional responses in our own bodies (plus, the neighbors won't be too happy about it). By the time frustration and embarrassment set in, they have pulled us off our center, and we find ourselves out of balance. From here, we can learn to return to the present.

Leading by example is the best method.

As our emotional state colors our every experience, dedicating a few minutes a day to our mental health through meditation can transform our whole lives. We all experience complex emotions and the impulses that come with them. Whether it's stress at work, irritation in traffic, or frustration about our dogs' behaviors, taking the time to put ourselves in a down-stay is a crucial part of leading our dogs and leading our own lives.

By working on our emotional stability, we can respond more appropriately to the needs of our dogs. When our dogs are stable, we can play our roles with greater ease and contentment.

CHAPTER 7

# The Mirror

Self-awareness is one of the most influential, yet under-emphasized aspects of dog training. When I first began training Lala at the beginning of our relationship, I noticed how tense I got when I saw anything that might trigger her. My heart raced, and my voice became harsh. Before she would even see anything, I was already anticipating the worst. Was she the reactive one, or was I?

During dog-training sessions, I began to learn more about myself—my emotions, thoughts, and reactions. Seeing Lala gallop about joyfully while I sat in vexation, it became clear that my frustration stemmed from my own level of expectation. While reflecting on each moment of her reactivity, I saw that I had a choice: to be honest with myself and see things as they were, or ignore what was going on beneath the surface. It would have been all too easy to point the finger of blame at her disobedience, the man with a beard and hat, or her potentially traumatic past that I had no control over, but none of those factors would have encompassed the whole truth. I could have thought that I was doing everything right, and my dog was not responding to my efforts.

But I realized it *was* about me, because of me—who and how I was in those moments—that I was struggling to reach Lala the way I wanted. It had to do with how I was showing up as a leader, how my expectations were affecting what I thought training was "supposed" to be, and how my shortcomings were getting in the way. Lala's eyes became a mirror that reflected my inner state back to me. I learned that a well-trained dog is only as good as its handler. Effective leadership requires that I be self-aware enough to catch myself when I'm leading poorly or allowing unchecked emotional reactions to direct my behavior.

Learning these key lessons, along with insights from my meditation practice, changed my whole outlook on dog training.

Even to this day, I understand that I must be aware of my emotional state while working with any dog, especially Lala. I always encourage my clients to be mindful of their own internal responses during training sessions. While dog training, we continuously observe everything arising in our dogs, ourselves, and the outside environment.

## Communication and Trust

Remember, our dogs' behavior is an indication of where the balance in the relationship happens to be. As we work with our dogs, we challenge them to perform new tasks or learn new behaviors, while also challenging ourselves. Although some dogs will have a natural propensity to learn certain behaviors or tasks readily and excitedly, many times, dogs will initially resist the training, especially when we push them into unfamiliar and uncomfortable territory. If the dog isn't resisting the training to some degree, then we are probably not effectively expanding their comfort zone and truly setting them up for success in the real world.

Training essentially involves creating a foundation of communication to guide the dog through stressful situations in a structured, functional, and appropriate manner. This approach teaches our dogs to handle the stresses that exist in real life. Without implementing stress in methodical doses, our dogs become emotionally fragile and cannot adapt to the chaotic world around them. By systematically and strategically introducing stress, we can help our dogs to become emotionally resilient in even the most challenging life situations.

Training builds an unconditional trust between the dog and the owner.

As much as every dog will thrive in certain aspects of training, they will struggle in others. Handling these difficulties head-on is the best way to train a dog. Although it can be less stressful and sometimes more fun to work on the areas in which the dog is proficient, if we fail to strengthen our dog's weaknesses, we risk creating an unstable foundation of trust and communication that becomes shakable in high-stress situations. We cannot ignore these shortcomings for long, because eventually conditions will arise that push the dog outside their comfort zone.

Before becoming a professional trainer, I trained Lala to do many cool tricks, some of which were somewhat functional. In low-level distractions, she excelled, and training was always fun. But when any of her triggers appeared, such as large men with beards, hats, or glasses coming within a hundred feet of us, she would react aggressively out of fear. These sudden outbursts were a reflection of exactly where I had failed to work with her. Although Lala had a deep understanding of the mechanics of the training we worked on, her ability to emotionally prioritize my guidance in medium- or high-stress environments was severely underdeveloped. These cracks in the foundation of our relationship caused us both to suffer.

## Thresholds, Responsibility, and Self-Awareness

It is crucial to identify the thresholds of the dog's comfort zone, how they behave in and out of these familiar territories, and how to expand these preferable conditions appropriately over time. Working on the dog's weaknesses in formal training settings is the best way to prepare our dogs mentally and emotionally for the unpredictability of life outside the safety of structured training.

At the start of my professional training with Lala, I used the down-stay as a structured way of increasing her stress thresholds. By introducing distractions at escalating levels, I was able to make Lala bulletproof in her ability to handle stress.

First, I put her in a down-stay with her leash and collar on, either in the middle of a room or on her dog bed. Then I took a metal trash can and began to bang it around from across the room. To ensure her long-term success, I needed to give Lala some wins before pushing her too deeply into stress, beginning from a far enough distance that she was uncomfortable but could still maintain the down position. After a few seconds of banging, I put the trash can down, walked over, and praised her. I communicated that when she heard loud noises, the appropriate thing was to trust me and follow commands. I then picked the trash can back up, getting closer and slightly louder. If she stayed, I repeated the praise. But if she failed and got up or ran off, I picked up the leash, popped the collar to communicate that her decision was wrong, and brought her back to the spot. (In a city full of loud noises and chaos, I needed Lala to remain composed so I could keep her safe.) From there, I would begin across the room again, starting from the beginning to give her another few wins. After several minutes, I would end the session by releasing her from commands and playing with her in celebration as she shook off the stress. I continued with this exercise with any distraction or trigger I could think of. Within a few weeks, I was able to slam things on the floor right next to her, ring the doorbell, and have people approach her, all without her reacting to her fear. I was finally seeing the emotional transformation we had been working toward.

It wasn't the mechanics alone that created the emotional shift in Lala; by using obedience training as a language, I was able to work with her emotionally, giving her clear feedback based on her impulsive reactions. Eventually, I could ollie (jump) over her on my skateboard or have her remain in a down-stay in a crowded dog park or outdoor mall. One vital factor to note is that in all my shenanigans with down-stay, never once did I let anything happen to her. I made sure each repetition ended on my terms, with both of us safe.

I introduced the stress, and I took the stress away.

Our successful training built an incredible foundation of trust between Lala and me. She began to have faith that if she experienced stress, I would guide her through and out of it effectively. Using this principle of relying on structure to acclimate her to stress—which can be applied with any obedience command, such as a heel position or sit command—Lala became the unshakable dog she is today. Instead of tolerating her actions and diverting blame onto everything I couldn't control, I took responsibility for her behavior and her emotional state and found ways of working that allowed us to transcend the limits of our old relationship.

When we become tolerant of our dogs' misbehavior, we become stagnant within ourselves.

I've encountered many owners who are too comfortable letting their dogs misbehave or act out, even aggressively, without recourse. It can be difficult to emotionally acknowledge our dog's unwanted behaviors once we have become passive in dealing with them. This passivity usually indicates our own emotional unwillingness to truly step up to the challenge of moving through any issues that may arise.

It is often easier to attribute unwanted and dysfunctional behavior to the outside influences in the environment than to accept our responsibility in the given situation. In a healthy and balanced relationship between dog and owner, the owner's influence over their dog should supersede the majority of environmental distractions. Instead of waiting until the trigger becomes too stimulating for the dog, we can begin taking action to acclimate them to stress now, in training, and set them up for success in the long run. Instead of blaming the environment (other dogs, people, loud noises, etc.) for any misbehavior that may occur, we can choose to take ownership of these cracks in the foundation of our relationship. These behaviors that we often sweep under the rug are the best teachers if we're willing to look at what they reflect back to us.

If unwanted behavior does arise, we may react with frustration and disbelief because of our selective ignorance about what our dogs are truly capable of. Many times, I've experienced owners downplaying their dog's severe behavior issues as a quirk or an anomalous event. We tend to create conceptualized images of our dogs in our mind's eye, picking and choosing attributes, yet often disregarding or ignoring certain underlying qualities that, to us, don't represent who we feel the dogs *are* in their essence. We must candidly bring our projections into our awareness to have a fully-realized relationship with our dogs. Without our self-awareness, the dogs will always be at the mercy of our ignorance. Although acknowledging what has been "under the rug" can be difficult, it is up to us to shed light on every part of our dogs, especially the shadows.

We can use our dogs as a mirror to reflect our responsibility in the situation.

On an episode of the *No Bad Dogs Podcast,* the trainer and monk Brother Christopher of Monks of New Skete discussed the connection between his spiritual life and his relationship with the dogs he trains. "[D]ogs [are] an amazing agent for insight into ourselves... for self-knowledge... They reflect us back to ourselves in ways that don't always happen in our human relationships." By developing a sense of awareness in dog training, we may see "some pretty sobering insights," such as "[our] self-centeredness, [or our] emotional imbalance at times."[7]

These insights can be powerful catalysts for change in our lives, in addition to how we relate to our dogs. We can use these insights to become better dog owners, friends, and human beings. Brother Christopher continues by saying, "When we cooperate with the dog and accept the responsibility, all of a sudden the relationship becomes something that is hard to describe." It becomes a doorway into a deeper relationship with our dogs, and with life itself. It becomes spiritual. It can shift our perspective from our egocentric thinking to the interconnectedness of all things in life (yes, including our dogs).

## Meditation and Interconnectedness

Dog training is a form of meditation, an insight into ourselves, and a deep spiritual practice—whether we are aware of it or not.

Training a dog can be emotionally challenging, and if we are not aware of our mental state during training, we can inadvertently project our negative emotions onto our dogs, damaging the relationship and pushing us into an unbalanced state. We can experience these unbalanced emotional states no matter how enlightened we may feel. Frustration and other negative emotions are natural responses to complex challenges. When our reality does not meet our expectations, this creates a strong energy current in the body. We can feel it tangibly as tension radiating up through our abdomen and into our sternum, shoulders, jaw, and temple.

How we manage this energy is crucial.

In my experience working with thousands of dogs and people, we sometimes inadvertently direct this energy toward the dog, instead of harnessing it to explore deeper and address the root of the challenge, which lies in our perceptions and expectations. During these times, we can realize that we, the humans, have also fallen out of balance. Once we realize we have lost our emotional composure—in the turmoil of feelings—it's time to put down the leash, end the training session, and meditate on our responses.

It doesn't necessarily mean sitting on a cushion in front of an altar or chanting mantras. We can at least stop to be still and reflect. By observing our behaviors and reactions, we can bring our best selves into training every day. It is fundamental to the art of dog training to contemplate the challenge in front of us more carefully, including looking at how our disposition contributes to the equation. Unless we can assess the impact of our behavior in different circumstances and develop a habit of regular introspection, these moments of unchecked frustration can lead to physical or emotional abuse and seriously damage the bond with our dogs.

When we develop a deep level of self-awareness and bring it with us into each training session, dog training can be a mirror into our behavioral patterns and shortcomings. Without self-awareness and sensitivity to the subtle energies between us and our dogs, we will never be able to guide the relationship into balance or help our dogs progress appropriately. Our projected frustration, anger, hopelessness, or anxiety will break both the dog's spirit and our own, throwing the relationship off-balance. The goal of training is never to break a dog's spirit, but to intertwine our spirits, forming one of the most ancient and primal bonds in the history of our species. I encourage you to challenge yourself to cultivate this self-awareness when training your dog.

Be ready to take a hard look in the mirror each time the leash goes on.

Each training session is an opportunity to learn many lessons for both our dogs and ourselves. We can look deeply into the mirror of our relationship, pushing out of our comfort zones, and continually growing and venturing deeper down the path of love and connection. In the process of cultivating a healthy and balanced relationship with our dogs, we hone our self-awareness to develop a healthier relationship with ourselves, and in turn, we expand this awareness into other aspects of our lives.

Just as we can train our dogs to be better, we can be better people and create a better world around us.

## CHAPTER 8

# Impulse Control

Impulse control and emotional self-regulation are essential elements of a healthy and balanced life for dogs—and for ourselves. Due to the ever-changing nature of our environment, we should cultivate an adaptable emotional landscape in our relationship with our dogs. A dog that has the emotional maturity to adapt to its environment will be far more emotionally stable than one that cannot. Regulation of emotions leads to healthier levels of decompression time throughout the day.

Think of impulse control as a mental muscle. To gain the fortitude to handle life's stresses, we work with our dogs to build this muscle over time. Taking on too much stress too quickly will leave the dog overextended, while too little stress will cause the muscle to atrophy. To build impulse control is to build emotional resilience.

As with humans, emotional resilience is the key to a stable dog.

Dogs aren't the only ones that benefit from impulse control and a little decompression. In my meditation practice, I have learned how impulsively driven I am. I'm often carried away by obsessive thoughts, some seemingly positive and others anxiety-inducing. When a thought arises about a particular subject that I'm passionate about or afraid of, my mind will latch onto it, diving down a never-ending rabbit hole.

After some time, I may return to the present moment and awaken to what has been happening. I see my agitated mind racing down different pathways as if there was something to obtain or achieve. If only I could think the right combination of thoughts, maybe I would feel content. Before I began meditating, these thoughts consumed my entire life. Rarely was I fully present; I lived as if through a veil.

## Mental Patterns

Through meditation, I began to recognize the underlying blueprints of these mental patterns. The process begins when we experience a sense perception. It could be a sight, sound, feeling, smell, or taste. Depending on the sensation or thought and our past conditioning, it will trigger an emotion. It could be fear, joy, nostalgia, anxiety, guilt, or shame. If it's a positive emotion, the mind will crave more and begin generating thoughts to try to latch onto that feeling. When we crave something, we emphasize the disparity between our desires and reality, putting happiness in an ever-elusive future, which inevitably causes suffering. If it's a negative emotion, the mind sees this as an urgent problem to solve. One thought leads to another, and with the next comes another emotion, and the mind rambles on as if there is something it must do about these feelings. The enlargement of our problems in our mind's eye doesn't leave much room for gratitude or compassion. We feel suffocated by the presence of this ever-expanding vicious circle.

The more intense the emotion, the more the mind scrambles to try to remedy it.

These bouts can last moments, minutes, hours, or even days, with no pause for clarity and calm. When we eventually do experience a lull in our thoughts, it can be surprising to realize how wrapped up in ourselves we have been. These impulses can dictate our mental patterns and, in turn, our actions, if we let them.

This process is laughably similar to the predicament our dogs are in when practicing the down-stay. One moment, Lala may be lying down and dreaming happily, but with only the crinkle of a bag of chips, her heart is racing, her pupils are dilated, and her mouth is drooling. The average dog may find themselves sniffing around the kitchen before they've even noticed that they're off their bed. I equate our dogs' urges to get up from their down-stay to my impulse to check my phone. Oftentimes, I'll be scrolling through social media without realizing how I got there in the first place. There must have been an urge from a thought or feeling, however subtle, that caused me to dig into my pocket and mindlessly open my phone, enter my passcode, open an app, and begin ingesting the content.

To regain agency in our lives, we need to learn how our impulses work. The moment we notice ourselves going down the rabbit hole is a moment of pure awareness. When we begin meditating, at first, we will become aware when the storm of thought and emotion causes us to suffer. It is the suffering that awakens us to what we've been doing. As we progress down the path, we will become more intimately familiar with the mind as it runs its course, and we will be able to catch ourselves sooner in the process. With time and experience, we will learn to recognize the moment when a thought, emotion, or urge arises. Once we are attuned to this level of subtlety, we can decide to choose a different, more appropriate path. We can see which thoughts and sensations lead to unwholesome action and suffering, and which patterns bring about wholesome action and liberation. By being present with our experience, we can take greater care in selecting which thoughts and experiences we want to give our attention.

## Self-Regulating

Even when not meditating, we can practice mindfulness of our impulses.

When an aspect of the world triggers us, with enough practice, we can continue to choose a path of compassion and kindheartedness. When we get cut off in traffic, can we see that we're all stuck and suffering together, or do we take it personally and honk and scream? When stressed after a day of work, do we go straight for a drink, a cigarette, or a spree of mindless social media scrolling, or can we see the self-harm and choose a healthier form of decompression? Without building this foundation of awareness, we are without agency, a victim of the world around us and our past conditioning. By working with our urges and impulses, we develop an ability to self-regulate and better adapt to our environment emotionally. These choices are far more difficult to exercise in the thick of our daily lives, but spending time meditating in the comfort of home or the tranquility of nature will help prepare the mind and body to thrive wherever we find ourselves.

A human learns many tricks throughout a lifetime.

We can drive cars, write books, build skyscrapers, and win gold medals in numerous sports. With the right conditions, we can do anything we put our minds to, as long as our emotional state is well-regulated. Without this regulation, we are liable to fall victim to lapses in mindfulness that can result in unwholesome behavior or speech.

I become most aware of these lapses when I'm driving in the notorious traffic of Los Angeles. No matter how Zen I may feel before merging onto the freeway, before long, my thoughts and speech often become competitive or hostile. Even if I don't mean it or there's no one around to hear me, I'm sometimes surprised by my judgmental thoughts in the heat of rush-hour traffic.

Dogs can also learn many things in the right environment, which needs to include building the ability to self-regulate and control impulses. Otherwise, these tasks lose their functionality when they need them most.

## Performing Under Pressure

Teaching a dog to understand a command is easy. Training a dog to perform that task or command under pressure or in a distracting environment is difficult. Creating an understanding of a command is different from being able to implement that understanding, especially in challenging circumstances. Without testing our dogs' ability to perform under stress, we are not truly training. To bring functionality and depth into training, we need to introduce stress in structured and strategic doses. We don't have to wait for the stress to sneak up on us when we least expect it and when we are unprepared.

A dog knowing how to sit for a treat in the home with no distractions is different from a dog being able to sit and stay calmly in a heavily distracting environment. I've encountered many dogs that can sit, high-five, roll over, and lie down on command in their homes, but the success rate drops drastically when in crowded parks or coffee shops. The purpose of training is not to show off how our dogs can follow commands for our ego's sake, but to be able to successfully bring our dogs with us to the most chaotic environments in our daily human lives.

Before we can expect our dogs to be Zen masters in a crowded public space, we need to start building this impulse control at home with the down-stay. In down-stay practice, we begin to condition our dogs to have more appropriate reactions to their urges. Each time their urges arise, we teach them to relax and remain nonreactive. In essence, we are saying, "When you feel fear, excitement, hunger, or any other emotion, don't get up, just lie there. I will take care of it, whatever it is."

Sometimes I wish someone would tell *me* that!

## Decompression

It may not happen immediately, but with repetition, our dogs will learn to relax and decompress in the down-stay. Decompression is an emotional state with nearly nonexistent impulses, resulting in a calm mind and body. By structuring time to decompress, we can condition our dogs to relax and become less reactive. Dogs will occasionally fully relax on their own (some more than others), but I often see dogs that have developed neuroses because their hyperactivity won't allow them to decompress. They fluctuate between a neurotic state and sleep with little in between, which is an example of a mentally unstable dog. We don't have to wait for our dogs to become unstable. Instead, we can practice our dog meditation, the down-stay, to allow our dogs adequate decompression time.

As our dogs get better and better at settling into decompression, momentum will build. Their impulse control will get stronger, and things that once triggered them will now seem unimportant. This momentum is a sign of progress. From here, we should see this impulse control permeating into other aspects of their training. They may be less reactive on walks, calmer in public, or less jumpy around people. When that happens, we can begin to take training further and continue to step outside our comfort zones.

For our training to be successful outside the home, our dogs need to become familiar with their urges and develop a strong ability to experience them without taking action. The dog must feel the impulse and allow it to pass. That is a tall order even for us. During our excursions into the world, inevitably, something will cause strong urges in our dogs. Food spilled on the ground could trigger their appetite, or the deafening roar of a passing school bus may send them into an anxious tailspin. These moments will test our influence and the dog's impulse control. If we are attuned to the dog and their emotional state, we can often see signs of these urges arising before they act on them. This level of awareness gives us a massive advantage in communicating with our dogs to traverse these stressful moments successfully.

Whether it's training the dog or training the mind, it is wise to be attentive to the subtle urges that may arise, learning to allow them to pass without acting on them. Instead, we can continue to choose love and compassion for ourselves, our dogs, and everyone else around us. Sitting on a meditation cushion (or a dog bed) allows us to use our impulses and urges as a medium to build impulse control and self-regulation.

## CHAPTER 9

# Tackling Situations Head On

Allowing your dog's unchecked, inappropriate behavior strengthens the behavioral pattern. When our dogs exhibit behaviors, such as barking, aggression, or anxious aversion, they are having an emotional, behavioral reaction to triggers, whether they're barking at neighbors, lunging at another dog, or fleeing from the sound of fireworks. It is difficult to know how to deal with these behaviors, particularly with anxious dogs, and we often hesitate to intervene appropriately. However, intervention *is* necessary. Behavioral issues are always best addressed head-on.

## Appropriate Intervention

Intervention allows us to interrupt the deeply ingrained neural pathways that create negative behavior patterns. This interruption will allow space for us to introduce a new, more appropriate response to develop. If we do not intervene, we leave our dogs with a false sense of how the world works. For example, when a dog barks at the delivery person, the delivery person proceeds to leave. For you and me, because we have a deeper understanding of the bigger picture and the way society works, we understand that these two things are unrelated. But to our dogs, they seem inseparable; they appear to be cause and effect. Our dogs develop the belief that the delivery person left *because* they barked. The barking scared off the potential threat—the delivery person—and protected the pack from possible harm, thus the instinctual response garnered the desired result and should be repeated should the dreaded delivery person dare return.

When such situations recur, this belief becomes more deeply ingrained into the dog's psyche. The dog has learned that barking is an effective and appropriate response to anything new that may be potentially threatening. Our dog will attribute its well-being directly to the behavioral patterns. Barking at the delivery person affords them the luxury of living in this house and keeping their pack safe. Dogs don't necessarily narrativize these situations—it's more of a reaction based on direct experience and feeling—although that is the closest possible human translation.

When we intervene in the unwanted behavioral pattern, we shift our dog's understanding of the role they play in the pack. With intervention, we don't allow our dogs to react unchecked, and yet the delivery person will still leave. Now the dog has encountered a different equation. She didn't utilize her defensive tactic of barking, and yet the threat—the delivery person—still left, and the pack remained unharmed. The dog must experience this alternative scenario many times before they will relinquish their urge to address the situation and eventually stop barking at the delivery person. Nevertheless, proper intervention ultimately teaches dogs that our leadership brings about a higher quality of life, because now they have less responsibility and, ideally, less stress and anxiety.

An excellent way of working with these dysfunctional behaviors is through structured training activities. Oftentimes, these triggers arise as we are going about our days. So, we are unprepared and therefore forced to react to our dogs' reactivity, which quickly becomes a big mess with little or no positive outcome. Instead of waiting for the triggers to sneak up on us and hoping that we will respond appropriately, I find it incredibly helpful to set up scenarios when we have the time, energy, and emotional wherewithal to handle the situation appropriately. Using the example of the dog barking at the delivery person showing up at the door, instead of waiting for their arrival, we can have a family member or neighbor ring the doorbell to trigger the response when we are prepared to deal with it. Adding structure, such as a down-stay, will dramatically increase the level of communication and understanding between you and your dog, which improves the likelihood of a successful outcome of the activity. By approaching the situation more intentionally, we get to practice how to respond appropriately to these situations when they happen, setting us and our dogs up for success in the long term.

## Responding to Triggers

When we work proactively and take the initiative in working with our dogs' difficulties, it proves to our dogs that it is *our* decision-making, not *theirs*, that maintains a high standard of living. We can apply a similar formula to a plethora of behavioral issues in a myriad of situations. The key is having a structured way of guiding our dogs through their reactive episodes by consistently repeating clear and direct intervention. Dealing with these issues in a structured environment sets them up to succeed whenever these triggers inevitably appear unexpectedly in daily life. Without developing a practice that we can build upon over time to eventually address the major behavioral issues, we cannot hope to overcome them in a lasting way. By building and maintaining a foundation of trust and communication, by developing influence, we can structure our dog's interactions and begin tackling issues head-on.

Our dogs aren't the only ones with illogical triggers and anxiety responses.

When I started my business as a professional dog trainer, I was broke. I couldn't afford anything beyond essentials, and even then, I had to borrow money from friends and family to cover rent, food, and gas for my car. Those circumstances, coupled with being raised with the generational frugal values of grandparents who lived through the Great Depression, created a certain mindset of scarcity for me. Any purchase greater than ten or fifteen dollars would cause me to obsessively contemplate my finances and, inevitably, become anxious. I am grateful that today I no longer have such dramatic economic constrictions. That said, I still occasionally get twinges of anxiety when I make an unnecessary purchase.

When that happens, the feeling is buyer's remorse on steroids. Even the purchase of a beverage in the middle of the day will sometimes cause me to reflect deeply on how much I've spent that month, how much I've made, and what my budget is, which causes a pit in my stomach, nausea, and, in some cases, even dizziness or an adrenaline rush. Again, thankfully, I can now afford a three-dollar beverage without it affecting my ability to feed myself and my dogs, pay my rent, or run my business. However, when my body and mind still occasionally react as if there is a current threat to my physical well-being, it causes me deep and unnecessary suffering. Reflecting on how my parents and grandparents manage their finances, it may be a generational trait.

I recall a moment when I started working with these feelings. I was new to Los Angeles and working a minimum wage job at a dog daycare. On my lunch break, I usually got a sandwich at a nearby Subway. On that particular day, I ordered the cheapest sandwich on the menu, and the cashier even gave me his employee discount. The sandwich was under three dollars, but when I tried to pay, my debit card declined. As I walked out hungry, I started to laugh because it was the exact situation that my anxiety desperately pushed me to avoid. I reflected on how it felt to be completely broke. I laughed because I didn't feel any less happy or dignified. I realized that my suffering over small purchases didn't mean anything. There I was, without money to buy lunch or pay rent, but all of a sudden it wasn't a problem. My mind let go of the narrative that money is the only thing saving me from total annihilation, and I enjoyed the walk back to work. I even enjoyed the hunger, oddly enough. I felt grateful that I had a job, a car with a quarter tank of gas, a few weeks before rent was due, and the best dog in the world to share it all with.

It's natural for us to experience such feelings in various ways from a variety of triggers. The trigger might be financial, as I've observed in myself, or it could come from our family history or intimate relationships, our dogs, politics, the traffic, or countless other things based on our conditioning. Unless we address the underlying cause of this anxiety, these emotional thought patterns will continue to persist and may even grow stronger. Even if we can't remove a particular trigger from our lives, we can still move beyond the dysfunctional emotional reactions that plague us and disturb our peace of mind. I couldn't remove the fact that I had no money, but I could choose how to respond to it. When we have an emotional response, we can choose not to react to it or give it the energy it needs to persist. That does not mean we suppress the feeling, but instead, we allow it to come and go, being aware of the thoughts without identifying with them, feeling them without acting on them. Over time, as we stop feeding these thoughts, they will begin to release their hold on us, until eventually, we are unaffected by them.

Moving beyond our "behavioral issues" takes courage, self-honesty, self-awareness, and most of all, self-compassion. We can use mindfulness and meditation, among other spiritual practices, to become intimately familiar with these alternative reactions to the way we experience stress. Looking deeply at and being present with our triggers of anxiety can be scary, and most of us would prefer to pretend they don't exist. However, ignoring them makes us more vulnerable and fragile and even more susceptible to the trigger than if we acknowledge and face it. We demonize our experience and begin to fear our fleeting feelings. Sometimes, even when the real thing isn't present, just the thought of our trigger can send us into a spiral. With awareness and honesty, we can begin to see the dysfunction in our reactivity. With courage and compassion, we can sit with our emotions, allowing them to run their course. On the other side of this emotional turmoil, we can see these bouts for what they are—old thought patterns that can't hurt us—and discover other aspects of ourselves to love.

Another trigger that I've experienced in my life is seeing a Nissan Altima because my ex-girlfriend used to own one. Seeing this style of car would evoke extreme somatic responses. It may sound ridiculous, but for months after our breakup, I used to get legitimate panic attacks every time I saw one. For whatever reason, I would see them everywhere—like, seriously everywhere. I felt haunted by them to the extent that I wrote a poem about it as a way of organizing and acknowledging my feelings. The fact that I would see them everywhere (at least ten per week) gave me many opportunities to work with my experience and begin to familiarize myself with those feelings. Using my then-newfound approach of mindfulness, I was able to slowly regulate my response to seeing a Nissan Altima and cease being ensnared by the anxiety that would always follow. Years later, it feels almost comical to write about, but it goes to show how conditioned these reactions can be.

## Weathering the Storm

When we are triggered and our genuine emotions reveal themselves, we need to learn to sit with them and become friends. Rather than running away every time they arise, we can invite them in. During meditation, we can seek out these reactions and remember to keep our composure, staying grounded during challenging moments. In Buddhism, we call it "weathering the storm." Using our breath as a focus, if painful and uncomfortable feelings arise, we can breathe through them and take refuge in our breath to ground us as our emotions kick up dust and create a storm of thoughts. If we take these thoughts seriously and begin acting on them, we can often make things worse. However, for those times when our emotions and thoughts are running wild with anxiety and worry, Zen master Thich Nhat Hanh offers his wisdom in his book *Being Peace:* "We do so much, we run so quickly, the situation is difficult, and many people say, 'Don't just sit there, do something.' But doing more things may make the situation worse. So you should say, 'Don't just do something, sit there.' Sit there, stop, be yourself first, and begin from there."[8]

We can find it challenging to remain still, inside and out, when the storm arises. We view our emotions as a problem to be solved, and we have a deeply ingrained belief that our *doing* will somehow alleviate these feelings. Our mind will tell us that if we keep doing something, eventually *something* must work and "fix" this feeling we're having. The problem is that our mind has a limited perspective and can never fully comprehend the entirety of the situation. Any action we take in this frantic state will leave traces of that energy in the result of the action, creating more problems in the future.

For instance, when we react to our dog's behaviors from an emotionally unstable place, such as yelling at them out of frustration, instability will seep into our relationship, even if the dog adjusts their behavior momentarily. That approach will cause a fear response and result in more difficulties in the future. Bringing peace to ourselves and the situation does not mean that we should remain entirely passive in our lives; it means our priority is peace. Undoubtedly, we need to address our dog's misbehavior by setting a clear boundary. Still, we can understand that the priority is to foster a healthy relationship and address the issue from a place of emotional stability. Finding our center and bringing peace into our decisions and actions is of the utmost importance.

Moving beyond the patterns and habits that cause so much unnecessary suffering means following advice that our intellect would not usually encourage us to take. As Thich Nhat Hanh says, "Don't just do something! *Sit* there!" That is precisely what I'm asking my dogs to do when I tell them to sit. In this way, I'm using our language of training to work with them emotionally. Often the most appropriate response to an impulsive emotion is to do nothing and let it pass. We must train ourselves, our minds, and our hearts to weather the storm and find peace and calm among all of our triggers, emotions, and chaotic thought patterns.

By sitting and practicing in a structured way, we can learn to handle ourselves with dignity and composure in even the most turbulent of emotional storms. We become the eye of the storm, witnessing our emotional turmoil from a grounded place. We can begin by practicing with small feelings, such as minor frustration or irritation, dull pains, or awkward discomfort, slowly building up to the more profound and complex emotions, such as grief, depression, rage, fear, hatred, and apathy. By moving slowly and becoming gradually more acquainted with unpleasant feelings and emotions, we build emotional resilience as well as confidence in ourselves and faith in our practice, enabling us to stay present and grounded throughout the unpredictable throes of life.

No matter how much we try to micromanage our lives and keep everything in its "rightful place," life has a way of throwing the meanest of curveballs. As Viktor Frankl wrote in his personal account of surviving the holocaust, *A Man's Search for Meaning*, "Forces beyond your control can take away everything you possess except one thing, your freedom to choose how you will respond to the situation. You cannot control what happens to you in life, but you can always control what you will feel and do about what happens to you."[9]

Similarly, we need to help our dogs manage their anxiety, reactions, and responses to various triggers. Stress is an unavoidable part of life for us and our dogs, so learning to move through stress tactfully becomes imperative in our process of self-evolution. Training our dogs, similar to training our minds, is an emotional journey of transforming these responses to generate more emotional stability and resilience.

Learning to proactively respond to life healthily, rather than reacting impulsively, is a crucial part of personal growth, spiritual growth, and being fully human. It's also a valuable aspect of how we care for our beloved dogs. Rather than suppressing our emotions and feelings, we should find ways to take the initiative and work with them, so we are stronger and more open-hearted on the other side. In this way, we can be a beacon of light, demonstrating courage. We can help guide ourselves, our community, and our dogs, creating a better world, filled with peace, love, and compassion.

CHAPTER 10

# Consistency is Key

As with any skill, mastery requires commitment to the craft and consistent practice over time. When we bring the training into our daily lives, we establish a level of consistency that our dogs can rely on and relax into. Mastering our relationship with our dogs turns everyday circumstances into opportunities to practice, improve, and grow.

Building habits and skills that allow for a greater quality of life takes time and patience, which means working with our dogs every day in some way, shape, or form, to reaffirm the boundaries. We need to practice those skills repeatedly in various environments until they become second nature. This process can often be painstakingly tedious and can seem daunting after the initial honeymoon phase of training has worn off.

## Training is a Journey

Most people who decide to train their dogs will show up enthusiastically and go through training for several weeks or months before losing the initial excitement and the consistency needed to create lifelong habits and behaviors. If I had stopped training Lala after getting a reliable response to a sit or down command, I would have never been able to share with her all the epic, adventurous experiences we have had together. I had initial goals, but as we grew together, I continued to see where we needed to progress.

Training is about the journey of maintaining balance, not about reaching any specific destination.

I always tell my clients that we don't intend for the training to be a few weeks of fun that eventually ends, after which things go back to the way they were. Instead, it is about creating and reinforcing boundaries and communication. Our dog's behavior is a reflection of our discipline as their handler; without this discipline, we won't be able to build the long-term habits we truly want for ourselves and our dogs. If we can't cultivate these qualities within our lives, we can't expect our dogs to behave any differently.

There is no destination in dog training, because training is about building and sustaining a healthy, balanced relationship with our dogs. Similar to working out or developing any skill, when we fail to be consistent, our results suffer. I always contextualize dog training as building the tools to maintain a relationship, because all healthy relationships take maintenance.

## Maintaining the Relationship

Without maintenance, relationships deteriorate over time. I would know. While I was successfully building my relationship with Lala, my relationship with my girlfriend was deteriorating, and I didn't even see it coming. I started to take her for granted, expecting her to meet my needs without me considering hers.

Without awareness of our pendulum's swing, we fall into habits that throw us off-balance. I was off-balance, and I didn't even realize it. I was constantly on edge, trying to force my way toward some mind-projected idea of success in the future, not realizing that in doing so, I was failing at most of what was happening in the present. I painfully learned that to find true success I need to be much more self-aware of what is going on around me, in my relationships, and also within myself.

We need this same awareness between us and our dogs. We can ask ourselves:

- How are we affecting our dogs?
- What are they trying to communicate to us?
- What do our actions communicate to them?
- Are we aware of how we communicate information to them?
- What are the subtle ways in which our energy and emotions affect the connection?
- What is the emotional state of our dogs?
- Are they in control of their impulses?
- Why are they acting out?
- Are they exhausted or overstimulated?
- Are we meeting their needs?
- Which needs may be unmet, and how might that affect their behavior?
- Have we thought about what's going on in their minds?
- Are we too narrowly focused on ourselves?
- Do we give up too easily because we are confused, embarrassed, or frustrated?
- Is our lack of consistency causing our dogs' erratic behavior?
- Do we feel overextended and overwhelmed?
- What structure can we add to generate more success in training?
- Have we prioritized training or do we fall back on old habits?
- How can we be more intentional in creating more consistency in our communication?
- What alternative approaches could we take to set our dogs up for success?
- Are we lacking patience?

There is so much to explore in our relationship with our dogs, and the key is to be consistent, every day and over time.

## Soul-Searching

Are you up for some soul-searching in your journey with your dog?

Within my practice of meditation, I find that consistency tends to reap greater rewards than the length of any individual session. If I meditate five to fifteen minutes each day, without missing a day, I find a greater sense of balance in my daily life than if I meditate for several hours on the weekends but forgo the practice during the week. Through daily practice, I continually remind myself of my aspiration to bring peace and love to myself and my community. When I fall off my routine, I notice that I am more likely to allow my emotional state to become unstable and affect the rest of my life. When I skip a few days of meditation, I can feel my old mental and emotional habits begin to come back. These habits are strongly ingrained and difficult to break, much like the instinctual drives of our dogs.

My journey of self-exploration was originally a way to develop a fresh and new relationship with life that brought me joy instead of anxiety; however, as with training our dogs, this relationship takes regular maintenance. My goal in meditation is not enlightenment. Instead, when I meditate, I aim to sit in stillness and do my best to be present, accepting whatever mental, emotional, or physical challenges arise. My work can often be incredibly stressful and demanding, causing frustration and anxiety that I would never want to take out on my dog or my family. The more regularly I practice, the better I show up for myself, my dog, and my community.

Consistency of meditation over time deepened my connection to myself.

Initially, I realized I was unskilled and needed training in living contentedly as a happy human: to love fully, cultivate joy and universal compassion, and bring these qualities into the rest of my life, especially to those I love, including my dogs. In the past, I had experienced glimpses of love and joy but didn't have the agency to cultivate these feelings intentionally, especially when conditions were undesirable. Being stuck in my selfish thoughts limited my understanding of the needs of my community, which in turn limited my ability to bring love into my everyday interactions consciously.

As I began to practice meditation, I had sincere realizations and insights about myself, my values, and visions for my life. As I explored the nature of the self, I began feeling a deep sense of peace within. At first, I could only find this feeling through meditation. I was calming my mind, and healing years of emotional suppression, getting out of my head and into my heart and body.

To actualize my values of self-growth, I realized that I had to develop self-discipline even in the most trying times. When I experienced profound heartbreak, I noticed that my relationship with my dog suffered greatly. My grief so consumed me that I neglected to prioritize quality time with my dog. I couldn't process the unpredictable nature of reality in a healthy way. I had never learned how to deal with turbulent emotions. I knew I needed to learn how to experience joy and peace even with the inevitable pain of loss that comes with being human.

With consistent practice, I noticed that the calm state I experienced following meditation was gradually touching other aspects of my life. It was a gradual process that unfolded naturally as I kept meditating and making a conscious effort to stay centered throughout my days.

I realized that even though I couldn't control the world around me, I could have more agency and influence over my emotions and my reactions to my environment. I realized that inner peace and happiness were not dependent on my external circumstances, but on my perception. As I implemented my new value systems, I began to address the unhealthy mental habits that I once identified with. I no longer desperately sought to control the outcome of every little action or agonized over every detail. I stopped believing that with my limited perspective, I could somehow consider every variable in any given situation and know how to manipulate each one to bring about my desired outcome.

I began to let go.

I started to see the freshness of the world again, and with that, I saw shifts in my relationship with the world around me. My situation was no longer an enemy to struggle against, nor a puzzle to solve, but a friendly reminder that there was always somewhere I needed to grow. As cliché as it may seem, I began to appreciate the little things again, which brought peace and joy into the mundane. Things that usually would have irritated me now seemed inconsequential, even comical. My mental health became a priority, and trivial incidents became less of a nuisance and more of a curiosity. More than anything, I began to take responsibility for my emotional state—without blaming my unhappiness or stress on everything but myself.

Meditation allows me to reflect deeply in my present moment experience.

My mind is now less judgmental and negative. Where there was once an incessant stream of neurotic thoughts consuming my entire attention, now there are gaps of space between the thoughts. Before I had the experience myself, I first learned about it from Eckhart Tolle's book *The Power of Now*, in which he writes, "Glimpses of love and joy or brief moments of deep peace are possible whenever a gap occurs in the stream of thought."[10] Now, when the thoughts occur, I am less engaged with them and ultimately take them less seriously. I am calmer even in situations that would have previously caused me immense stress.

I still experience stress. However, I react less to the rise of adrenaline and cortisol and respond more from an inner sense of freedom. In all, through consistent practice, be it meditation, yoga, dog training, or any other path of mindfulness, I find myself better able to deeply connect with my present moment experience, allowing me to show up as my best self for my dog.

The commitment to self-growth is rooted in consistent discipline.

Bringing our practices into our daily lives is a crucial step to bringing about lasting results in training our dogs or our minds. Despite our good intentions, implementing training unskillfully or inconsistently can create suffering for ourselves and those close to us, including our dogs. When we develop the ability to be consistent, we give ourselves a refuge from our experience of difficulties and stress. We can bring balance back into our lives and create space for insight, which can lead to a deep understanding of ourselves, our dogs, and the world around us. Cultivating the life that we want with our dogs continues long after the training session ends and spills into every waking moment with our canine companions.

## CHAPTER 11

# Letting Go of Expectations

Oftentimes, we expect our dogs to be on their best behavior, which would create the least conflict in our current situation, but we have failed to create the conditions to make that possible. It's similar to expecting to achieve incredible physical shape without exercising or eating healthily. We may want our dogs to stop pulling on the leash, but we have never taught them how to walk nicely. We may wish our dogs would stop barking at the window, but we haven't given them an alternative outlet for their energy. We want our dogs to be friendly and well-mannered, but we haven't shown them how to socialize appropriately. We want our dogs' behaviors to be predictable and reliable, but we haven't implemented enough structure to make that possible.

## Managing Expectations

We need to learn to manage our expectations throughout the training process. A dog may exhibit desired behaviors one day, yet behave entirely differently the next. That can be frustrating and confusing for a trainer or owner, but it is not an indication that the dog has regressed in their understanding. Generally, the cognitive understanding of what we are asking our dogs to do is not the issue; it is our dogs' trust in our ability to guide them that will fluctuate, depending on how regularly we set and maintain boundaries. Poor behavior from our dogs reflects an imbalance in the relationship rather than the dog's inability to comprehend our verbal cues. Many people believe that training is a set period with a finish line, that once we've achieved a certain level of obedience, it will never waver, but that is not the case.

When training our dogs, it's best to address the immediate needs of the situation without throwing too many of our expectations into the mix. Many of us have an agenda with our dogs in training, on our walk, and throughout our day. We have an idea—an expectation—of how the interaction will be and feel. Inevitably, reality shows us the hollowness of those expectations. For example, an off-leash dog runs up to you during a training session; a group of skateboarders flies by during your peaceful walk; or the delivery person rings the doorbell when you're trying to relax. Be willing to throw your expectations out the window at a moment's notice.

Without being able to see our expectations as mental fabrications that may have little to no bearing in reality, we often react with emotional instability, acting out our resistance to what is happening, which makes stressful moments more intense. When we catch ourselves thinking, "This shouldn't be happening," that reveals our expectations. Adding frustration or anxiety to the equation won't allow us to address the situation any more readily and will often lead to even more dysfunction. By letting go of our expectations, we come into the present moment and handle things appropriately without bringing our anger, fear, or disappointment into the situation. Although we may have an assumption about how each consecutive training session will look and feel, a surrendered, present mind is the ideal condition for the best possible result in any situation with our dogs.

### Working with What Is

Recognizing and appreciating the unique individuality of humans and dogs, and the bonds between them, is an integral aspect of dog training.

No two people are the same, and likewise, no two dogs are exactly alike, and the dynamics in any relationship are unique. By respecting, accepting, and embracing the individuality of our dogs' expression and our own, we can build the healthiest possible dynamic with our four-legged friends. When we can see ourselves and our dogs exactly as we are—strengths, weaknesses, and everything in between—we can observe how our natural temperament may be getting in the way of creating a compatible situation with our dogs. Without this honest acceptance, reality (and frustration) will inevitably conflict with our preconceived notions. With honesty, bravery, and enduring commitment to our dogs, we can grow to be the person they need us to be.

I encounter dog owners who subconsciously, or blatantly, want to change their dogs' underlying personality without even considering making a change to their own. That is a futile effort. We cannot change a suspicious, introverted dog into a happy-go-lucky extrovert, or a hyperactive working dog into a couch potato, no matter how hard we try. Learning how to manage our expectations and honor the unique personality of the dog in front of us is a crucial aspect of connecting.

Instead of trying to cram the infinitude of reality into our narrow perspective of preferences, I suggest that we accept our situation and work with what is right in front of us, exactly as it is. From here, we have an opportunity to work with what we have, instead of fighting against it (either physically or emotionally). We may need to accept responsibility for our behavior and shift how we interact with our dogs to better meet their needs. Seeing our dogs for exactly *what* they are allows us to meet them exactly *where* they are and bring them through training to achieve a deeper sense of balance and harmony.

As my pack grew over the years, I had to grow with it. Having five dogs of all different sizes, breeds, and temperaments added an entirely new dimension to dog ownership and training. Since they are each unique, I need to treat them differently to achieve a standard level of behavior and obedience with all of them.

Yogi, my Belgian Malinois, was the third addition to the pack. I found him chained to a tree in the jungles of Oaxaca, Mexico. He came to us deathly emaciated, happy and jovial, but lacking in confidence. We smuggled him back to Los Angeles as a service dog, knowing that he needed veterinary care. As we nursed him back to health through months of heartworm treatment, he gradually came out of his shell. He's a shy and nervous dog that craves guidance, but he's also very well-behaved on his own as he craves our approval. He enjoys structure and needs little reinforcement within his daily life to abide by our house rules.

Peanut, my Pomeranian, is quite the opposite of Yogi. He is a spicy, little guy that loves to break the rules. He came to us from a family that had neglected him. He was left at home alone in an apartment for most of his days, and even when he did have company, he didn't get the engagement he needed. When surrendered to us at two years old, Peanut came with every bad habit in the book. He learned through experience that negative attention is better than no attention at all. Being smart, he used his intelligence to get into whatever trouble he could for the connection he desired. He would constantly pee in the house, steal food right off my plate at the dinner table, bark incessantly, and steal my socks, to name a few examples. He even bit my finger, tearing it open, as I pulled chocolate out of his mouth. His journey through training was arduous, as he required more structure and training than any dog I've ever worked with to create conditions that made him tolerable to live with. I recognized his deep desire for interaction and began teaching him advanced service dog tasks to meet his intense drive. He excelled in training, and several years later, he and I are inseparable, and our bond is unlike any other I've had with a dog. (That being said, he is still just as devious and rambunctious as ever. His intelligence has not diminished.)

If I had treated Yogi and Peanut the same, we would all have suffered. If I had been too lenient with Peanut, he would have ruined my life and gotten himself killed (I'm only half-joking here). If I had been as strict with Yogi as I am with Peanut, he would have shut down completely. By responding to precisely what the dog is giving me and being willing to question my expectations, I'm able to tailor my training to the dog in front of me and set us all up for success.

## No Bad Dogs

Although a dog may exhibit bad behavior, there are no *bad* dogs. Peanut is not a bad dog, no matter how poorly behaved he may be. All unwanted behavior is an opportunity for dog owners to teach and consequently bond with their dogs. We will all undoubtedly have days of disappointment when it comes to our dogs' behavior, but we must not be discouraged. We must refrain from projecting the identity of "bad dog" onto our dogs because our projections will only color our experience and limit our ability to see clearly. A moment of weakness does not define the dog. We should recognize that each incident of bad behavior is not a regression in our dogs' learning, but rather an opportunity for growth. Our reactions to these behaviors are of the utmost importance. Instead of reacting with frustration or exasperation, an attitude of curiosity and inquisitiveness can be much more productive in growing the relationship—a lesson Peanut continues to teach me every day. With a sense of deep awareness, we soon see how our dog's emotional state and behavior mirror our emotional reactions. Although an unfathomable number of factors influence our dog's behavior, we must be aware of the most crucial influence: ourselves.

Many dog owners will look outside themselves in hopes of finding the root of their dogs' unwanted behavior.

I was guilty of doing that myself with Lala when she was young.

How could I expect my dog to be focused and present during a training session while I was frantic and scattered? How could she trust me if I didn't know how to handle myself and manage her in certain situations? How could she relax if I was always focused on getting to the destination, rather than being present with this step in the journey? When I recognized what was happening and honestly reflected on such questions, everything changed.

What I didn't know initially was that Lala's triggers were not the problem. The problem was my lack of influence with Lala, which was a crack in the foundation of our relationship. She seemed reasonably well-trained at that time, but as soon as she was fearful, I lost all my influence over her. That was a clear sign that our relationship lacked the trust and balance we needed to handle the stresses of our daily routine. She was emotionally fragile, unable to handle the stress of normal life, and she lacked control over her instinctual impulses. Over time, I learned the importance of my emotional reactions and expectations. Instead of scratching my head over her specific triggers, I built—and continue to maintain—a foundation strong enough to handle whatever arises, even the biggest triggers. Now, Lala is more confident and more emotionally resilient than ever, which enables us to have the best adventures together, free from any unnecessary stress.

## There is No Finish Line

There is no endpoint in dog training, which is the same for our path of growth.

There is never a point where the relationship will stand on its own without putting in the work. Zen master Thich Nhat Hanh gives us this wisdom when he writes, "You follow the North Star, but your goal is to get back home; it's not to arrive at the North Star."[11] We can have a vision of our perfect life with our dogs, but it is equally important to realize that our goal is not to arrive at perfection; it is to create balance. Similarly, in our own growth journey, we may have a vision of our ideal self, but whether we achieve it is inconsequential. By bringing awareness into our lives, we do our best each day, getting better little by little, striving to restore balance in our lives.

Through dog training, we see reflections of our own paths to growth.

A culture of quick fixes and a need for immediate validation cultivates impatience and despair in us. We face numerous methods of addressing these anxieties, fears, and insecurities in our turbulent times. Aside from more destructive choices, such as turning to drugs or alcohol, we may go on hikes or bike rides, do yoga, write in a journal, meditate, hit the gym, read a book, train our dogs, learn a martial art, play the guitar, or go skateboarding or surfing to help alleviate our suffering. My primary practice is meditation. I have talked to so many people who tried meditation a few times, expecting to find instant serenity and, unsettled by the restlessness of their own minds, never returned to it.

Psychologist and Zen practitioner Barry Magid, in his book, *Nothing Is Hidden*, wrote, "[T]he path of realization is anything but linear. Zazen [sitting meditation]... is not a means to an end."[12] Without understanding our underlying feelings and motives, it is easy to get lost in our expectation of how meditation is supposed to feel, instead of observing our immediate mental and emotional landscape exactly as it is here and now. Magid goes on to say, "Our path will start with whatever curative fantasies we harbor and it will meander through many byways of trial and error as we slowly, reluctantly come to face life as it is."[13] With awareness, we can purify our meditation practices of our tainted expectations, rooting ourselves in the step we are taking right now.

This approach also applies to other practices. When reading a book, we enjoy taking in each idea and thought of the author; we don't race to the last page as a finish line. In martial arts, we don't train every day in hopes of earning a black belt, but to hone the craft and perfect the art. On a bike ride, we don't have to always focus on getting from point A to point B; we can become immersed in each beautiful passing moment, unconcerned about our destination. Pure practice has no goal. Pure practice has no concept of gaining or progress. It is a means and an end in itself. When we sit, we do so with no other intention than to sit, curious and welcoming whatever arises.

In practicing meditation, similar to training our dogs, we sit and observe the experience of sitting in our bodies and minds, whether it aligns with our expected direction or not. Although it sounds simple, we can find it challenging to face insecurities, boredom, or restlessness. Fortunately, we are still making progress when we repeatedly experience the same complex emotions on our path. Insights may need to come many times before they transform our being.

Dog training isn't all sunshine and rainbows; the same is true of our path of self-growth.

As much as we may prefer things to fit within the box of our expectations, the human experience rarely does. Although our ideas of meditation probably involve some deep tranquility and transcendent states of consciousness, oftentimes we just sit with last night's argument on repeat in our heads, or fantasizing about our weekend plans, or ruminating about the aches in our backs and the noisy neighbors. The quality of our meditation is not determined by whether we enjoyed it or it matched our expectations, but by our commitment to being with whatever presents itself. We may imagine feeling blissful and calm during meditation, and sometimes that happens. In reality, we can often feel raw, vulnerable, and terrified. When we are in the heart of a complex emotion, we can feel confusion, discomfort, and as though we are lost. These feelings are part of the path and as valuable as a moment of clarity or resolve. The idea of a predictable path is only a concept, a construct of the mind to help us feel more in control of the uncertain experience.

Practicing the spiritual path is about learning to work with ourselves, exactly as we are, similar to how training dogs is about working with them exactly as they are. Although we may have a vision for the kind of person we aspire to be, spirituality is about honoring our experience right here, right now. Jesus or the Buddha may inspire us by their example, and for our dogs, we may imagine them with traits similar to Lassie or Air Bud. However, comparing ourselves, or our dogs, to seemingly unattainable goals can be deflating and painful. Still, we don't completely discard our aspiration to grow into our best selves and help shape our dogs into their best selves. Instead, we continue on the path with the understanding that we intend to grow, not to become perfect.

Breathing mindfully in and out, we make peace with ourselves, our dogs, and the world around us, exactly as everything is in the present moment, wherever we may be on the path.

## CHAPTER 12

# Reactivity

Dogs communicate with us every second of the day and, whether we realize it or not, we are also communicating with them. In addition to our conscious communication that creates stability, unconscious communication allows our habitual emotional reactions to dictate the energies between us. Everything we do throughout the day, every interaction we have with our dogs, communicates with them on some level. It can be obvious and intentional, or subtle and accidental.

Regardless, we react to the communication we receive. If your sleeping dog suddenly jumps up from the dog bed, obviously on high alert, barking with fixation at the door, would you react? You would likely have an initial emotional reaction, such as a spike of adrenaline when your body activates the sympathetic nervous system. Then, using this sudden burst of cortisol, you would take action to address the situation. Taking a deep breath, you get up and check the door, or you may angrily yell at your pup, assuming that she disturbed you over nothing. Whatever your response, it communicates something to your dog, even if it's unintentional.

Oftentimes, when you yell at your dog, however cathartic it may feel, you are communicating your emotional instability, which won't instill a sense of trust and security in the dog. Your dog may be fearful of your change in tone and cower under a chair, or, because of your instability, she may continue spiraling into a frenzy of barking, feeling that the initial outburst was appropriate. There is a back-and-forth exchange of energies that communicates how we should both react. Our natural response may not always help achieve the desired result.

I always encourage my clients to be proactive, not reactive.

## Being Proactive

Don't wait until you are frustrated or emotionally compromised to implement structure, communication, and discipline for your dog. Unconsciously taking our frustration out on our dogs damages the relationship we are working so hard to foster. If a dog barks incessantly while we are trying to relax, our initial impulsive reaction might be to yell at the dog out of frustration. That approach may get a moment of silence, but the yelling will elicit a fear-based response that will not create lasting communication, respect, or positive behavior. Our frustration is not useless; it can be beneficial as an indication that we are off-balance—a signal that our usual way of dealing with the dog's behavior is not working. We must change our behavior to achieve a different result. Allowing oneself to feel this frustration in its entirety, without instinctively acting upon it, can inspire us to build more structure and better communication with our dogs.

We can begin to work on behaviors with our dogs before we become emotionally compromised, and stay one step ahead instead of one step behind. Remember when we discussed using the down-stay to help with specific triggers? We can use structured training exercises to work on areas where the dog struggles behaviorally. Working on difficulties on our terms gives us the time and emotional wherewithal to handle them effectively and appropriately.

Dog owners who are aware of their fluctuating feelings will establish healthier relationships with their dogs more quickly and smoothly than dog owners who are oblivious to their shifting moods. Dogs can pick up on how people feel, especially their owners, and will react to these changes. That reality became apparent to me early on in my career when I worked with one of the most aggressive dogs I have ever trained, a German Shepherd named Charlie.

## Developing Trust

In dog training, our goal is to create a foundation of understanding and build a relationship in which the dog learns to use their drive to work with us instead of against us. Charlie's exceptionally strong instinctual drive, even at eight months old, made training more difficult because it created massive resistance against everything that I tried to teach him. His behavior was skittish and feral, yet he displayed confidence with his bark and bite. He viewed me—and anything related to training— as adversarial, something that he needed to resist and fight against. Charlie had an instinctive tendency to lunge and snap aggressively every time I challenged his understanding of appropriate behavior by setting boundaries for him.

For example, in teaching dogs to walk with the leash loose by my side, I set a boundary that they must not walk ahead of me. Each time the dog passes me on a walk, I change direction with a light pop on the collar. With most dogs, the abrupt change in direction generally startles them and brings their attention back to me. Then I motivate them back to my side and praise them enthusiastically. This feedback challenges the dog's understanding, then introduces and encourages alternative behavior.

Charlie's reaction was distinctly different.

Every time there was tension on the leash, whether created by me or not, Charlie turned around and lunged with his teeth bared, snarling and ready to bite. I struggled with the leash, holding him away from me the best I could, sometimes with only a centimeter to spare, until he would eventually calm down. These incidents happened multiple times during every walk and training session. Each time, my adrenaline spiked and fear took over. He never successfully bit me, but even his attempts were incredibly intimidating. Each time I would take him out,

I was already anticipating the fight, and my anxiety would preemptively flare up.

At first, I seemed to be making progress, because Charlie was such an intelligent dog, but each day, even each walk, was different. Some days, we got through a training session, and I felt encouraged by his relaxation, but the next day he was attacking me again.

With the help and insight of some other well-respected trainers, I came to realize that my fear and reservations were impeding our ability to build mutual trust. Up until that point, I had worked with many aggressive dogs—the aggression is usually associated with fear—but never one this confident, intelligent, and calculated.

Charlie could sense my fear.

To him, that meant emotional instability, and a strong-willed dog will not trust an emotionally unstable leader. It didn't take him long to learn all the training commands, but he didn't trust me, and for obvious reasons, I certainly didn't trust him. I aimed to work with this dog so we could become a team, but how could I expect him to trust me when I didn't trust him? Even when he was calm, I felt on edge. I had to set aside my fear, frustration, expectations, and ego to focus on what was right in front of me and to stay in the present. Once I realized that, I was able to manage my fear and remain nonreactive. We were both agitated and stubborn, but I had to be the first to let go of the fear. I had to control my breathing and heart rate and concentrate on remaining calm while this aggressive dog was lunging, snarling, and snapping at me. It was up to me to deescalate the emotional tension. I had to take the initiative in breaking down the walls between us, knowing that he would not.

I had to be vulnerable first.

Practicing meditation to separate my instinctive response from outside stimuli, as well as sheer repetitive trial and error with Charlie, taught me to control my innate, fearful, adrenaline-rush response. I started before I would even put on the leash. I practiced several minutes of breathing exercises, slowing my heart rate and quieting my anxious mind. Once I felt calm and stable, I opened his crate door and reached in to put the leash on. The drama would begin as soon as we got out of the front door, as he anticipated the conflict. Each time Charlie lunged, I returned to my breath and remained nonreactive. I would de-escalate the situation and return us both to a calm state before proceeding. Each aggressive incident became shorter and less dramatic until they dissipated almost entirely. I had to prove to Charlie that I would not back down and would not allow him to cross my boundaries (I'm not a fan of getting bitten, and neither were his owners!). At the same time, I had to communicate to him that although I was firm, I was also fair, and all I wanted was to be friends. Even though the progress wasn't linear day by day, over the weeks he lived with me, we finally began to build trust. As a result, I could truly start bonding with him and cultivating an environment where I could help acclimate him to the stresses of our modern human life.

Working with a dog that has such intense energy and powerful aggression, I couldn't hope to fight against it and win. Reflecting on my true intent, I realized that my goal wasn't to prove to this dog that I was bigger and stronger, but to give him a longer, more fulfilling life by training him to behave appropriately in his daily environment. Unfortunately, Charlie wouldn't last long in a shelter, which is where he was headed if I couldn't reach him. To deal with his aggression, I also had to show him there was a way for him to win. With the clarity from meditation and the setting aside of my baggage, I was able to work *with* Charlie, not *against* him, and he was able to work with me, not against me. We were able to connect. Instead of getting frustrated by the lack of linear progress, I could address whatever situation was in front of me without expectations of the path ahead or projections from past interactions. By understanding and accepting the reality of my circumstances, I could respond much more appropriately to the situation for the benefit of all involved.

Charlie and I developed a deep trust and a strong foundation of communication, which he brought home to his owners. By working with our circumstances and not against them, by practicing generosity, we become one with the situation and our growth.

## Intentional Communication

To gain influence and take leadership, we need to dictate the emotional energy and remain nonreactive to each challenge. The moment when our dogs become anxious, afraid, hyper, or even aggressive is the most crucial time to stay calm, confident, and steadfast in our leadership.

A true leader leads in every aspect of a dog's life.

In wolf and dog packs, the "alpha" never takes a day off, ever. Since we assumed that responsibility when we decided to integrate our dogs into our family, it is imperative that we demonstrate our commitment to our dogs constantly and consistently. Each time we allow a dog to misbehave, every time we give them too much slack, the underlying message we transmit is that we lack the conviction in our leadership to commit to reliability and trustworthiness. We must bring the subtle messages we send to the forefront of our attention to intentionally and intuitively communicate how we want the dog to fit into daily life appropriately. The more intentional our communication, the more we can cultivate the relationship.

For example, in the first few months with Lala, when I would put us in situations that challenged the integrity of our communication, I felt tension in my body and a sense of unease between us. When training off-leash in areas where the distracting stimuli around us superseded my influence over Lala, I found myself stressed and anxious; my heartbeat quickened, my senses heightened, and I scanned around for potential destabilizers. I communicated to Lala that I felt out of control, nervous, fearful, or upset, and she would respond with the behavior she thought was appropriate for the situation, perhaps attempting to take over the task of leadership, feeling herself a more fit leader in that moment. A tug-of-war would follow, escalating my frustration, and she would not understand why her response to my emotions was wrong.

An outburst would likely come next—hers or mine, or both.

The more tense I became, the less stable my emotional state, and Lala would become less and less obedient. If I became agitated, she became agitated. A strong leader remains calm and composed in the face of danger or chaos.

## Staying Calm

Thich Nhat Hanh describes this principle in his recollection of escaping a war-torn Vietnam in a small boat: "Often boats are caught in rough storms, the people may panic, the boat may sink. But if even one person aboard can remain calm, lucid, knowing what to do and what not to do, he or she can help the boat survive. His or her expression… communicates clarity and calmness, and people trust in that person. They will listen to what he or she says. One such person can save the lives of many."[14] When our dogs look to us for guidance and see emotional instability, they view us as less trustworthy to guide them through a chaotic experience. We may not be in a boat in a rough sea, but we can still be the calm one for our dogs. We can be the beacon in the dark to guide them safely and effectively through our turbulent modern landscape. If we are sufficiently quiet and still, centered inside our mind and heart, we can see our situation clearly, respond to it appropriately, and our dogs will trust in following our lead. Staying calm is the key to effective leadership.

When Lala and I were in a situation that played to our relationship's strengths, I would relax and enjoy the experience. After learning about the benefits of meditation and maintaining a consistent practice, as well as honing my skills as a dog trainer, I was better able to remain in control of situations that would previously have left me feeling unstable. My relaxed tone communicated to her that I had everything managed, so that she could relax too. She trusted that my commands would result in positive experiences overall. Even if I pushed us both outside of our comfort zones for a challenge and growth opportunity, I would regulate my emotions to show her that we were still safe and that I had things under control. If we encountered a rattlesnake during a hike, instead of freaking out, I stayed calm and recalled her tightly to my side, and we would choose a safer route together. Without my guidance, she might have kept running and exploring, unaware of the danger. By trusting in my instruction, she allowed me to keep us both out of harm's way. Whether it was a rattlesnake on a hike or a busy parking lot in the city, my leadership kept us safe.

Eventually, I felt as though she were an extension of my body, never doubting for a second whether she would listen or not, a clear indication of the balance between us. However, her response is not robotic and automated; it is precise and calculated, a result of the trust built through our practice together. When I finally learned how to quell my nerves under challenging circumstances, I could then successfully lead Lala through situations that would have previously sent us both spiraling into bouts of anxious reactivity.

I always encourage my clients to radiate calm, soothing energy to their dog, rather than letting their dog's frantic, anxious energy affect them. When we become compromised and are thrown off-balance, our dogs will also become unstable. The more stable we are emotionally, especially in a crisis, the more consistent our dogs will be in their behavior when we need it most.

## Moments of Contraction or Kleshas

In life, we all experience times when it feels as though our world is closing in on us and we get a sort of dense, stuck, depressed, claustrophobic feeling. I call these times of stress *moments of contraction*. When we experience loss or heartbreak, when the rug gets pulled out from under us and it seems we have no ground to stand on, life can seem bleak and terrifying. Our unconscious and unintentional tendency is to close off and withdraw into the shell of our egos. We contract or retreat into our comfort zone, becoming defensive and oblivious to the compassion and open-heartedness that we have worked so hard to cultivate, and revert to our habitual behavioral patterns.

Any action we take while we're in this state of mind will only create more problems for us. When we act out of jealousy, greed, anger, ignorance, or any afflicted emotional state, we risk reinforcing these responses in ourselves, and also risk projecting this negative energy outward to our dogs. Then, they reflect that negativity back on us through their responses. In reverting to old emotional habits, we risk setting in motion a vicious cycle of unhelpful stress-based reactions from ourselves and our dogs.

In Buddhism, there is a word for these states: *kleshas*. A klesha is a "hang-up" or an afflictive and unwholesome emotional state that limits mental clarity and our ability to stay grounded in our integrity. Mark Epstein, author and psychotherapist, defines kleshas as "powerful reactions that have the capacity to take hold of us and drive our behavior. We believe these reactions more than anything else, and they become the means by which we both hide from ourselves and attempt to cope with a world of ceaseless change and unpredictability."[15] When our unwholesome emotional states dictate our behavior, we cannot hope to create more peace and compassion in our lives and the world around us, much less effectively lead and care for our dogs properly. As we experience these moments of contraction, it is so easy to fall back into these states and manifest unwholesomeness. In those moments, and truly in every moment, we have a choice to either perpetuate the destructive patterns of ignorance or accept and be open to our immediate experience.

We can break the cycle with awareness.

## Deepening Awareness

Developing awareness is the key to breaking this destructive feedback loop that can cause so much of our suffering. We may not be able to control our emotions, our thoughts, or the world around us, but with enough practice, we *can* control our reactions to them. By becoming more aware of our mental and emotional landscape, we can discover the source of our unwholesome thoughts and actions. Awareness empowers us to see the emotions as they arise, observe them without impulsive reaction, and even watch as they disappear. We can intervene between the stimuli and our unhealthy responses to break the pattern and create space for a new and healthier alternative to develop.

Behavioral patterns can be so deeply ingrained that we can't see through them amid a storm of emotion. Developing a regular practice such as meditation helps to build emotional resilience, which allows us to stay calm and level-headed when difficult emotions overwhelm us. By actively working with our emotional state when life isn't too chaotic or heavy, we learn to trust in our ability to sit with our experience. By doing so, we develop the skills we need during moments of contraction. If we wait until the heaviness of life is upon us, we will find it is much more challenging to remain nonreactive than if we have developed a regular practice. By incorporating a practice into our routine, we gain a deeper understanding of ourselves and recognize our habitual reactions. As we navigate life, we can use these stressors and triggers as tools of awareness, beginning with minor, inconsequential situations and gradually building our emotional regulation so that we can handle the big stuff. We can't bubble-wrap ourselves, but we can cultivate a more stable grounding in our being, setting ourselves up for success as we experience the inevitable pains in life.

Begin to practice nonreaction when little things happen, such as when your dog misbehaves. Whatever emotion flares up, let it arise, notice it with gentle compassion, and refrain from acting upon it immediately. Inhale the feeling, invite it in, and do not resist it. Explore the sensations of the experience with curiosity. How does it feel? What is the texture or tone of the feeling? What is your initial impulse when it arises? Watch your mind race around, looking for escape routes or vices to cling to. Be vigilant of justifications for unwholesome reactions. Remain in stillness, giving the emotion space to exist and pass through. The more resistance you have toward the feeling, the more it can become stuck within you to cycle again and again. As psychologist Carl Jung proposed: What you resist will persist. By letting it pass through, by remaining nonreactive, you can truly let it go.

I've been practicing nonreaction for years, and I often laugh at the amount of frustration that small events can cause, especially misbehavior from Lala. Remember, Lala used to be incredibly reactive, and I used to be just as reactive in response. Even today, as perfect as Lala is *(and she is!)*, she could still use some improvement. Sometimes when I get caught up in my agenda for our training sessions and I omit allowing adequate time to warm up, Lala will falter and become disengaged, lazy even. Dogs can have off days too. To this day, my initial emotional reaction is frustration. I have to catch myself in that moment to realize the absurdity of my response.

Then I can laugh about it all.

By seeing the whole situation as it is, I'm able to address it with warm compassion for everyone involved. I see a dog who doesn't want to work, and is resistant to the idea of a hard training session. I see a guy who got caught up in his expectations and emotions and is taking it all too seriously, even though he's doing what he loves most. Beyond that, I see two beings on a big rock hurtling around a giant ball of fire in infinite space. What was so gravely serious about the training session that caused such a dramatic response? Nothing! How could I forget that the whole point is to simply bond with my dog and enjoy our time on this earth together?

If that isn't the human experience in a nutshell, I don't know what is.

As we become more aware and gain more influence over our emotional states, we learn to remain calm and confident in any situation. We still feel; we feel more deeply than before, but now we can be fully present with what we are feeling. Remember, frustration is a helpful emotion that signals to the brain that it needs to adapt and learn, and all emotions communicate vital information. The difference is that we can allow the emotion to pass without giving it any of our energy. We can learn from the emotion without resisting it or reacting to it. When we stop resisting our present-moment experience, wasting energy doing so, we experience a newfound energy with which we can move through these moments of contraction and kleshas more gracefully, making space for a new and healthier perspective and response to emerge on the other side.

Deepening our awareness and developing nonreaction allows us to fully accept our experience, whether we enjoy what is happening or not. It enables us to embrace the mystery and uncertainty of life with composure and confidence. With discipline and determination, these new habits will gain momentum until we remain effortlessly nonreactive to life's curveballs. We cannot expect our dogs to make this emotional transformation without us first making it ourselves.

CHAPTER 13

# Resource Guarding

Many of our dogs' instincts were once beneficial to the longevity of the pack when resources were scarce. But in our modern society, where we fill their bowls every day, instincts are often obsolete and dysfunctional. While scarcity still exists in many parts of the world and is experienced by both dogs and humans, now more than ever in history, many of us are able to feed ourselves and our dogs, fortunate to evade the scarcity our ancestors once endured. Behaviors that would serve the dog and its pack effectively in the wild have become a liability and a burden in our homes. When humans meet all of a dog's physical needs—food, water, and shelter—many of the dog's instincts cease to serve a purpose. Understanding these instincts and how we relate to them is an integral part of overcoming specific behavioral issues.

Training is a process of working with these instincts to create in our dogs a more functional, foundational approach to life.

## Instinctual Behavior

Resource guarding is an excellent example of a dysfunctional dog behavior that was beneficial before domestication. Also known as territorial aggression, resource guarding is a drastically misunderstood

97

behavioral issue that comes from an instinctual mindset of scarcity. As a professional dog trainer, I frequently encounter dogs displaying aggressive behavior, such as growling, snarling, or biting, to protect specific objects, food, or their owners.

Our dogs' ancestors needed to conserve resources at all costs.

Although these behaviors were historically advantageous for pre-human canids, in the modern context, they can be dangerously dysfunctional. When resources *are* scarce for dogs, guarding food can mean the difference between life and death for themselves or their pack. In our homes, when our dogs defend the stolen sock, favorite chew toy, or bone, these behaviors only cause dysfunction. Such instincts are so deeply ingrained through evolution that no amount of selective breeding can completely eradicate them. However, with clear communication through proper training, we can effectively address and alleviate these behaviors.

This resource guarding behavior can also be seen as a social display of dominance. If a dog feels it has the authority to decide who can and can't have a particular object or piece of food, that means the dog feels it has the right to control resource distribution in the pack. As a direct challenge to the pack hierarchy, it renders the structure of the pack unstable.

Aggression in any situation is a sign that clear boundaries have not been set or are not respected.

Another behavior that most dog owners would prefer to eliminate is prey drive—the intense drive to hunt for smaller, fast-moving prey. Sometimes we forget that our dogs are predators and carnivores. When we throw a ball or frisbee for them to chase, we are activating their prey drive. Even the squeaker toys we give them emulate the scream of a dying animal. In the wild, an intense prey drive is necessary for survival, but our dogs often key into this instinct in counterproductive ways. A dog inappropriately bolting after a squirrel on a walk is an example of prey drive. I recently worked with a dog that would literally drag their owners down the street to chase any cats or squirrels.

## Scarcity Mindset

We can observe a similar, yet equally dysfunctional mindset in ourselves, though it's subtler than a dog's instincts. The resource guarding and prey drive seen in dogs parallel the human mindset of scarcity—an instinct inherited from our ancestors. Peter Coyote, a Zen priest, actor, and narrator, alludes to this in his book *Zen in the Vernacular:* "To Buddhists, humans arrive in the world of form with evolutionary propensities for greed, hatred and delusion (qualities that perhaps once offered evolutionary survival benefits)."[16]

With a mindset of scarcity, our day-to-day existence is under constant threat. Anything outside ourselves is the enemy—predators, business competitors, or bacteria—and any perceived challenge to our needs is an obstacle to overcome. Our habitual attachment to stability, permanence, and security leaves us in a constant state of malcontent.

Similar to dogs guarding their resources, when we emphasize the feeling of separateness through habitual, egocentric thinking, the ego dominates. From this limited perspective, reality appears obscured, and we are unable to work with the situation in front of us to respond appropriately.

As Alan Watts captures in his Taoist philosophy: "The art of life is more like navigation than warfare, for what is important is to understand the winds, the tides, the currents, the seasons, and the principles of growth and decay, so that one's actions may use them and not fight them."[17] When we resist what we cannot control, the universe seems to work against us. By accepting things as they are and working with life—not against it—we begin to cooperate with the whole, using wisdom to interface with our experience in the most appropriate way possible. That will always net the best possible result, even if the mind and ego cannot see what that may be.

In times of scarcity, humans hoard what we have—which never seems to be enough. We become stingy and selfish, unwilling to give in fear that resources will run out. This is our instinctual "resource guarding." When a dog hoards and guards food in our modern world, it cuts itself off from the pack. When we adopt a mindset of scarcity, we cast aside generosity, perceiving it as irresponsible, which cuts us off from our community. Scarcity convinces us that greed and selfishness are a logical response to our predicament. Yet, in truth, we are not as separate from one another as we think.

Humans tend to identify with an ego—a mind-made sense of self. As Alan Watts explains, the ego "symbolizes the role you play... but it is not the same as your living organism."[18] The mind constructs a sense of "I am" based on conditioning. We do the same when we anthropomorphize our dogs, creating a mind-made identity of who we feel they are while leaving out whatever doesn't fit that narrative.

We may identify with our names, ages, genders, appearances, preferences, histories, nationalities, or even illnesses. Yet our egos often forget that our very survival hinges on countless factors beyond our control—from the quiet labor of our spleens and gallbladders to the vast mechanisms of global economies, food systems, and the delicate balance of atmospheric conditions that sustain life. Even our dogs and their behavior shape who we are. When we define ourselves based on our likes, dislikes, and conditioning, we forget that they are a collection of perceptions that we cling to so we feel a semblance of continuity. These perceptions do not represent the entirety of who we are.

By identifying with this concept of self, we divide the world into "self" and "other." Anything outside our barriers of skin feels essentially not "us." But these divisions represent only partial truths. Modern science shows the physical universe is an ever-evolving collection of atoms and molecules. Everything, including ourselves, is in constant flux. The self that we perceive as fixed and stable is always shifting and transforming in accordance with universal patterns of change and interdependence.

From the human perspective, we may feel separate from our surroundings. In truth, we are an integral part of the universal whole—an unfolding process far greater than our minds can grasp. When a dog feels it is a lone wolf and hoards resources, it forgets that it is a part of a pack and dependent on that pack to survive. An outlook of scarcity separates us from our communities and the universal play of life. When we recognize our inseparability from everything in the universe and transcend identification with the ego, we can see that by aspiring to serve others, we are also attending to ourselves.

## Abundance

A dog with abundance makes sure the whole pack is fed.

Abundance is the recognition of our inherent interconnectedness. It is the openness and receptivity to the universe itself that is the source of all abundance.

Addressing how we fundamentally relate to our surroundings will reveal how we operate within our environment. If we constantly fear and keep our distance from those around us, isolating ourselves and hoarding our belongings, we cannot hope to build healthy, deep connections. If we do not give ourselves entirely to our pack, our community, or our present moment, we deny ourselves the support of the universal process.

In the Bible, Jesus said, "Give, and it shall be given unto you." (Luke 6:38, KJV). The level to which we give of ourselves (and what we have)—to which we participate in the universal play—is the extent to which we will receive support in return. If we cannot embrace our experience, whatever form it may take, and if we constantly bring emotional resistance into each moment of our lives, we cannot accept true abundance.

A way to address this resistance is to ask ourselves, "Is there resistance in me?" or "What am I resisting right now?" Without thinking, we can sit in the openness of the question and allow the answer to reveal itself. We may be impatient, bored, restless, or anxious. Wanting to change how we are feeling brings resistance to these emotional states, and with it, suffering. Accepting how we feel in this moment allows us to come back into alignment with the Tao—the harmony and natural order of the universe.

All that ever exists is this present moment, and if we aren't content with what we have *now*, then we create suffering for ourselves. Finding peace has little to do with the content of our lives—our life situation—and everything to do with our *foundational* approach to life—our perspective. With abundance, we realize that we have everything we need to find peace and joy at this moment. There will never be a time in the future when *having* more brings us more happiness unless we are already happy with what we have right *now.*

Generosity is the cornerstone of abundance.

To be limitlessly generous does not mean to give when it does not mutually benefit those involved from a broader perspective, especially when giving can enable and perpetuate the receiver's suffering. As an ancient Taoist proverb says, "Give a man a fish, and you feed him for a day. Teach him how to fish, and you feed him for a lifetime." Teaching a man to fish may be more generous than giving him a fish. Teaching a dog how to exist appropriately in a given environment by setting firm boundaries can be more generous and compassionate than allowing them to persist in a folly that limits their quality of life. Saying "no" when needed can be an act of generosity. If we want to meet the needs of the whole pack, we must also consider ourselves. From a place of clarity, we can begin to be mindful of our generosity.

Transforming ourselves starts with how we approach life, a choice we must make in each moment until it becomes so natural that we exude abundance everywhere we go. We turn external circumstances into allies, regardless of how desirable or undesirable our minds perceive them to be. Essentially, we choose to befriend life in whatever shape or form it comes in, the way a Golden Retriever gives and welcomes affection from anyone, no matter their look or personal history.

In training our minds, as in training our dogs, we shift our perspective toward abundance and rid ourselves of the mental blueprints that perpetuate our suffering. The decision is ours. We can choose scarcity, which the Buddhist monk Mingyur Rinpoche describes in his book *In Love with the World* as feeling "divided from ourselves and the world around us... the deceptive narrative of the grasping mind." Or we can choose abundance, from which "we can learn to let go of false hopes that leave us yearning for ease in our bodies and in this world...

We can replace longing with love… [W]hen you love the world, the world loves you back."[19]

Improving the quality of our lives means deciding to live every moment in abundance. We can choose today, right now, in this moment, to take an active role in addressing our attitude toward life and how we view ourselves and each other—and how we treat our dogs. We can strive to understand our canine companions and work toward living abundantly with them, thus increasing the quality of all our lives.

## CHAPTER 14

# Dog Whispering

One afternoon, Lala and I were at the park with some friends of hers: an older male White Shepherd named Zeke, a female German Shepherd named Lily, and a young male Border Collie named Otis—regular playmates of Lala's for several years. They all played so well together as we—the other owners and I—threw balls and frisbees, watching the dogs sprint and dance about in a truly beautiful display of proper socialized play. I had trained Lily and Otis years earlier and had become friends with their owner, a longtime friend of Zeke's owner.

I'd never formally worked with Zeke, though I spent considerable time with him in these informal settings. Zeke was wary of people and rarely, if ever, approached a human other than his owner. If a stranger were to wander too close to our play group, he would begin barking and positioning himself between us and them. Being at a public park, that was not appropriate behavior. Although I had known Zeke for several years and he no longer felt threatened by me, he never approached me, made eye contact, or initiated interactions. He always kept a healthy distance. Understanding his nature, Zeke's need for space did not bother me, and I respected his boundaries.

On that particular day, an unwitting couple approached Zeke. His prominent features and pure white coat are mesmerizing to onlookers. Zeke did not appreciate their unwelcome approach and began growling; his hackles went up, and he began slinking toward the strangers in an unfriendly manner. They did not take the hint and continued approaching. Zeke's owner, knowing his dog well and being responsible, immediately noticed the shift in his energy and began moving toward him and calling his name, but Zeke ignored and evaded him. I found myself in a position to intervene, and I reacted instinctively. I took a small, but abrupt step toward Zeke, cutting off his line to the couple. I heightened my posture and gave him a piercing stare, communicating that I had the situation under control. Zeke immediately went wide-eyed; his hackles went down, his posture relaxed, and he retreated. After a few words, the couple moved on, and our play date resumed.

Moments later, with the situation diffused and the couple long gone, I sat down on the grass, and Zeke came up to me and nuzzled into my leg. In the past, he hadn't so much as let me (or anyone else) even touch him, so to have him be open and affectionate with me on his terms was truly an exceptional experience. I took his behavior as an invitation, and I reached out slowly, beginning to pet him under the chin and chest. He raised his head and started licking my cheek. I couldn't help but smile; it was such a beautiful moment for me. I had finally earned Zeke's trust with patience, understanding, and clear communication.

Zeke's owner, surprised by the whole scene, especially Zeke's sudden affinity toward me, quietly asked half-jokingly, "Did you just dog-whisper him?"

I laughed and replied, "Yeah, I guess I did."

## Deeper Communication

One of the most common mistakes I see people make with their dogs is relying on verbal cues without laying a foundation of deeper communication.

What do I mean by "deeper communication"?

As humans, we rely almost entirely on verbal communication, at least as far as we're aware. Our thoughts come in the form of words and concepts. We prioritize one's "word" above all else, exemplified with colloquial terms such as "you have my word" or "a man is only as good as his word." I entirely agree that words hold incredible power in how humans communicate with one another. However, we often overlook deeper, non-verbal, universal methods of communication—things that slip past our conscious attention, yet we use them every day. Although these cues can be much more subtle than simple body movements, we typically refer to them as "body language."

Somewhere along the line of developing and prioritizing language, we, as humans, have forgotten the universal language of the body. Charles Darwin put it this way: "But man himself cannot express love and humility by external signs, so plainly as a dog does, when with drooping ears, hanging lips, flexuous body, and wagging tail, he meets his beloved master."[20] We can communicate emotion, elicit specific feelings, and cultivate energy using only the movements of the body. We can do so intentionally or unintentionally.

When we're communicating with our dogs, the most powerful language is body language.

Before moving into more advanced and complex methods of dog training, such as verbal cues and words, we can first communicate with them on a level that they innately understand. Although there is a considerable amount of overlap, dogs and humans consciously communicate on different planes. As a professional dog trainer, it is my job to develop a language that comes halfway between a dog's physical language and our verbal, conceptual language, allowing owners to communicate more effectively with their dogs.

The best approach to begin building this connection is to meet the dog on their level with physicality and body language. The idea that we can use words with dogs and assume that the dog will "figure it out" leads to significant gaps in the foundation of a dog's training. This lapse in communication confuses the dogs and frustrates the owner. It is easier for us to learn to speak dog than for dogs to speak human.

Therefore, it is our job to start teaching through physicality—the dog's language—before working up to the verbal cues of our language. Since most people don't already understand how to communicate with dogs using physicality, allow me to elaborate with a few examples. (Note that these examples will not apply to overly aggressive dogs that require greater expertise and finesse.)

## The Leash

First, we use the leash, the collar, and our bodies to show dogs the rules of the house and to create boundaries. Instead of waiting for the dog to violate one of our arbitrary boundaries and becoming frustrated, we need to clearly communicate what those boundaries are ahead of time and reinforce them, before a misunderstanding creates any dissonance between us. A dog will not understand our expectations without us first teaching them what they are.

We all have expectations of our dogs, even if we're not consciously aware of what these are. Alexandra Horowitz explains them in her book *Inside of a Dog*: "Many people's expectations, at least in this country, are fairly similar: be friendly, loyal, pettable; find me charming and lovable—but know that I am in charge; do not pee in the house; do not jump on guests; do not chew my dress shoes; do not get into the trash." We may have many unspoken expectations of our dogs, but "somehow, word hasn't gotten to the dogs."[21] It is not rational to believe our dogs will innately comprehend our expectations, so it is our job to make them abundantly clear to the dog.

The leash and collar are the best tools for communicating and establishing these boundaries. A leash, in addition to being a means of restraint, should always be a tool of communication. By leaving the leash and collar on at all times whenever dogs are free in the home, we now have a way to effectively communicate these boundaries to our dogs. If our dogs jump on the couch without permission, we can use the leash to guide them off. If we want to put the dog in the crate for the evening, we can guide them there with ease, rather than having to chase or grab them. The leash can even help us begin practicing down-stays. Leaving the leash and collar on communicates that we call the shots and puts us in a position to effectively show our dogs how to operate in the world around them.

Wearing the leash is similar to training wheels for our dogs. We shouldn't take off the training wheels until they've found their balance. Dogs learn how to operate in the world, whether we guide them through life or they guide themselves, relying on many obsolete instinctual drives, which generally result in unwanted behaviors. Therefore, we may as well begin teaching them exactly what we want, setting them and ourselves up for success.

With initiative and consistent reinforcement, we can guide our dogs to understand their place in our lives.

## Body Language

While body language is underappreciated, it is crucial for understanding physicality in dog training.

To demonstrate the power of body language, imagine a seven-foot-tall man towering above you, leaning over you, inches from your face. How would you instinctively react? Undoubtedly, your posture would shrink, and you would shy away. The alternative would be to push him away, but in either case, it will cause emotional discomfort and an instinctual reaction. That innate reaction to stimulus is not always conscious. The tall man leaning over displays dominant body language, while your impulsive reduction in posture would be submissive, and pushing him away would be responding back with dominant action. Body language is an integral part of many aspects of our lives, as it is for our dogs. When we're slouching, standing up tall, leaning on something, crossing our arms, or even the amount of eye contact we make, whether we realize it or not, we are constantly communicating to those around us.

A dog always communicates with others using its body. A well-trained eye can see anything you need to know about a dog within minutes by observing its body language. Subtle signs are often overlooked, and this observational skill takes time to develop. For example, how the dog wags its tail, the rate of the dog's breath, or the intensity of its gaze.

If we do not effectively lead them, dogs assert themselves in many ways that can often go unnoticed.

One can also look at a dog's ears, tail, or posture for clues as to how the dog is feeling. Ears pinned back indicate submissiveness, while ears pointed forward and erect mean the dog is alert and focused. Hackles raised are a sign of intense dominant arousal and can indicate a potential threat to others around. Dogs use their eyes and tails to convey different messages. The glazed eyes watching you eat dinner are far different from the piercing gaze of suspicion. The tail tucked between the legs means the dog is nervous and submissive, while the tail raised high is generally a sign of confidence. A wagging tail means the dog is excited. It's well known that a wagging tail can mean the dog is happy, but fewer people know that a stiff, rapid tail wag can be a threat of aggression. Understanding what a dog is communicating helps us know how they are feeling, specifically about the pack dynamic, or what's on their mind.

To notice these subtleties, we need to be aware of the dog's energy by looking at its body. How is the dog behaving? Frantically or calmly? Confidently or tenuously? Do they move with a relaxed grace or a stubborn tenseness? Do we see dominant behavior or submissive behavior? While *dominant* and *submissive* are clunky words to describe the observed behavior and don't capture the subtleties and nuances of behavior, we can discard any negative connotations and use them loosely in these contexts. Examples of dominant body language include leaning toward and over your dog rather than away from them, stepping closer to your dog as opposed to backing away, or remaining emotionally calm and collected while your dog reacts in distress. These dominant behaviors exude leadership and communicate that your dog can trust your guidance. Examples of submissive body language would be leaning away, backing up, positioning behind, or belly-up. There are appropriate and inappropriate times for both dominant and submissive behaviors from both ourselves and our dogs.

Although dominant body language is important in leadership, we can also use submissive behavior strategically to achieve certain results. To invite someone through a door, we step back and open up our hips and shoulders, allowing them space to pass. To be inviting to a dog, we can crouch down to become more approachable. Averting the gaze of a potentially dangerous dog or human communicates submissiveness, which is incredibly useful for avoiding unwanted conflict. While these cues may seem inconsequential to us, even the subtlest use of conscious body language can make a huge difference in communication with a dog.

To create as much clarity in our communication as possible, we should be aware of both how our dogs are behaving and our own behavior, as well as how the two are influencing one another. Are we leaning in or recoiling away? Are we standing tall or crouching down? Is our posture strong or weak? Is our gaze soft or glaring? Are we breathing heavily and rapidly or slowly and calmly? How is the dog responding to these cues? Is there anything we could do differently to achieve a more harmonious result?

## Position and Proximity

Physical proximity is an important factor in communicating with your dog. Dogs know that the further they are from you, the less influence and control you will have over them, and the less likely they are to be reliably obedient. It's much easier to recall a dog from two feet away than one hundred feet away. If a dog doesn't listen and obey commands reliably when the leash is on, then the owner should not be taking it off any time soon outside of the house (or even inside the house!).

Creating a solid foundation of training on leash sets a dog up for success when the leash comes off. Working off-leash reliably with a dog, which includes obeying a recall immediately, ignoring external stimuli, and prioritizing the owner's command, takes a tremendous amount of influence and a deep, trusting bond. Dogs must prove themselves reliable within the six-foot distance of the leash to set them up for success when they receive off-leash freedom. Long leashes and e-collars (when used correctly and under the supervision of experts) can be instrumental in maintaining structure and safety from a distance. Your ability to implement the same accountability and communication with your dog at a distance as up close allows the dog and owner to take the training and depth of the bond much further than working without these advanced tools and conditions. These training techniques build more trust between owners and their dogs, eventually rewarding the dog with more freedom to explore and express their innermost nature under our watchful eye.

Dogs use position to communicate as well.

Positional communication relates to where a dog positions itself during training. By studying the dog, we can gain insight into the dog's communication through its body language, both during training and in everyday situations. Being instinctually dominant, dogs will often wander out ahead of us and pull on the leash. From that position, we are essentially backseat drivers, which means the dog feels it has the wheel, in other words, the authority to make decisions for the pack, such as who to bark at, what to sniff, or what to eat. More often than not, dogs are purposeful with their movements as well as with their proximity to the pack, especially mature dogs, because that is how they communicate with one another. When our dog is ahead of us on walks, whether pulling on the leash or not, it is leading. From this position, our dogs are much more likely to become reactive or dismiss our guidance.

Without you building and maintaining structure, a dog will often pull ahead, asserting itself in the environment. That dynamic can be uncomfortable for both the dog and human, and can also be dangerous. I had a client who allowed lenient loose-leash walking. The dog wouldn't pull on the leash, but was always drifting several feet ahead. One day on a walk, a car ran a red light as they entered an intersection, and the dog was hit and killed. We were all heartbroken. But with a stronger emphasis on structure, they could have avoided this tragedy. With practice, we can establish a default structural position for our dogs to follow that is ever so slightly behind us. Commonly known as a *heel position,* it refers to the paws of the dog being positioned by the heel of your foot, as mentioned earlier. Even once we've established this position for our walks, dogs will sometimes position themselves slightly in front or even put a paw on your feet. Although it is subtle, the dog is demonstrating dominant behavior. When training and redefining the relationship between dog and owner, there can be moments where leadership is not clearly defined. By placing its paw on your foot, a dog expresses how it feels about the pack dynamic: The dog is willing to comply with specific commands, but hasn't fully accepted the structure and hierarchical roles. I interpret this behavior as the dog getting the final word in.

Another familiar example of positional communication in training occurs after you teach your dog a solid heel position in walking, when you stop and ask the dog to sit. Then, you can see the emotional state of your dog. If the dog doesn't stop, or stops in front of you, or even faces you but refuses to sit, that's a sign that they are not prioritizing your structure. Therefore, you are not in control, even when you may have thought otherwise. Most dog owners could lose control at any moment if their dog is only partially listening. By coming to a stop, you can check to see where the dog positions itself, which is a good indication of how much focus and effort the dog is putting in. A dog that stops with you, even slightly behind you, looks at you, and sits attentively is applying themselves.

Although we may not need one hundred percent effort from our dogs all the time, we should be aware of exactly how much effort is required for the dog to successfully traverse the given environment and prioritize training in the face of a potential trigger. Working with a dog to give consistent effort will set it up for success in difficult or dangerous moments. These signals from the dog are not good or bad, but they can be helpful in understanding where the balance is in the relationship at any given moment.

Oftentimes, when clients ask their dogs to go into a down position, they will back away slightly. That movement sends mixed signals to the dog because the down command is dominant. When asking our dogs to lie down, we are asking them to take a submissive and passive position, thereby taking a subordinate role in the pack's hierarchy. If the dog chooses to lie down on command, it follows that we assert ourselves in a dominant position in the pack. By giving a dominant command with submissive body language, such as backing away or bending away from the dog, you leave the dog to decipher your meaning, and it will often follow the body language instead of the verbal command. Alternatively, I suggest that clients lean into their dog and step slightly in front of their front paws. That may sound a bit ridiculous, but it is highly effective at creating clarity and aligning the messages of our bodies and commands. Try it for yourself and see what happens.

## Picking up on Energy

Beyond bodily movement, another, more subtle and deeper aspect of silent communication is our emotional energy. In my experience, as I've integrated more spiritual practices into my life, I've excelled at reading people. I attribute this ability partially to the expertise I've developed in reading body language from constantly communicating with dogs. Sometimes I can read people from the subtle energies that exist within the entirety of their self-expression—from their vocal tonality and inflection to their posture and movements, or their eyes. It is sometimes easy to tell whether someone is open and receptive or closed off and shut down by observing their micro facial expressions or nuanced body language. One's body can often give clues to the internal state, even when our words say otherwise. Humans can be deceptive in this way. Dogs, on the other paw, can only communicate authentically, as pointed out by Alexandra Horowitz: "Dogs are ingenuous. Their bodies do not deceive, even if they sometimes cajole or trick us. Instead the dog's body seems to map straight to his internal state."[22]

When we sit down to meditate, we become familiar with the energies that exist in our bodies. Similar to an antenna, we tune into the frequencies in our inner emotional landscape. Quieting our minds allows us to perceive what is beyond all the chatter, into the realm of silence. This self-awareness is more profound than any thought we could think. It is our intuition and our deepest self: who we are beyond our conceptual thinking. Once we have felt our energies, we can begin to attune to the energies of everything around us, sensing our interconnectedness with the universe.

When we prioritize verbal communication and thought, we often lose touch with deeper levels of connection, as seen in how people in our culture communicate with dogs. Much subtler is how we as humans communicate and connect. The most valuable connections are often silent. Fred Rogers of *Mr. Rogers' Neighborhood* spoke on this issue when he said, "Our society is much more interested in information than wonder, in noise rather than silence... And I feel that we need a lot more wonder and a lot more silence in our lives."[23]

In working with dogs, we need to understand what dogs can and can't infer from our communication. This attention will help us best direct our energy toward building the relationship we (and our dogs) truly want: one that is free of tension, anxiety, and frustration. Dogs will respond most effectively and appropriately to physicality, body language, and energy.

As we grow in self-awareness, we can communicate our message more intentionally. Effective communication with our ancient brethren, our dogs, starts with relearning to use our bodies more purposefully. The better we understand one another, the better we can communicate. The better we can communicate, the deeper our connection will continue to grow.

CHAPTER 15

# The Dynamic Dog

As a dog trainer, I see dogs differently than most people do. In addition to what I see right in front of me—the dog in its current mental-emotional state—I see the potential of the same dog when taken through the transformational progression of training. Many owners can't see the potential in their dog. They deal with and tolerate inappropriate behavioral issues due to a lack of understanding of the relationship from which these issues arise. They don't know that a life could exist without these behaviors, and identify their dog according to the behaviors rather than seeing the behaviors as symptoms of an unhealthy or imbalanced emotional state. Although we can tolerate some unwanted behaviors on the surface, when we look deeper, they often indicate psychological distress. These owners will benefit from learning about communication for building a healthier relationship with their dogs.

I recently worked with a Labrador mix named Dixon that would completely lose himself anywhere near a squirrel. During our most recent session, we, along with my five dogs, began seeking out squirrels to test his resolve around such a challenging trigger. As we approached a group of trees laden with squirrels, Dixon began to fixate and drool, while my dogs relaxed calmly in the shade. My client noted that before our training, she would have dismissed Dixon's fixation and reactivity as normal dog behavior. But after observing how calm and uninterested my dogs were, she gained a clearer understanding of what appropriate behavior should actually look like.

Allowing our dogs to persist in their folly without our intervention sentences them to a lifetime of psychological instability.

Let's say we have a happy or excited dog—we'll call him "Fluffy"—that goes bananas every time it sees a dog or person, and shows no self-control, lunging, panting, and barking. Although we may feel that this excitement means Fluffy is happy and normal, we aren't looking deeply into the dog's state of mind and the underlying indications of instability. If we constantly allow the pup to indulge in this unchecked excitement, it will inevitably cause more problems than it alleviates. (Even in a curious, happy puppy, this response often leads to maladaptive reactivity in the long run.) A dog lacking the ability to contain excitement lacks the necessary impulse control and emotional self-regulation to exist functionally in our modern world. This emotional instability may be tolerable in certain situations, such as in the yard. However, in almost all other situations—on walks, at parks, in restaurants, at friends' houses, or anywhere else in public—the dog's behavior can become dysfunctional and inappropriate. We may say that it's Fluffy's personality and how he interacts with the world, but I believe this assessment sells the dog painfully short.

## One-Dimensional vs Dynamic

All dogs can regulate emotion and behavior if we show them how, expect it from them, and hold them accountable to these expectations. A dog that cannot cope emotionally with the reality of life around them and has only learned one narrow path of interaction with this reality is *one-dimensional*.

We must acknowledge that it would be better for all parties to have a more *dynamic* dog, one that can appropriately respond to situations as they come, without ever losing themselves in excessive instinctual reactivity. While fear reactivity is an example of inappropriate behavior we often encounter, I find excessive excitement to be similarly dysfunctional.

A friendly Goldendoodle that drags its owner down the street and lunges excitedly toward any dog or person to greet them is just as inappropriate as the Chihuahua that barks ferociously in fear. There are times when it is appropriate to allow our dogs to express these urges freely, and there are times when our dogs should exercise impulse control. In training, we build a relationship to guide our dogs to override these instinctual impulses, eventually with only our voice. A simple command, such as "easy," "gentle," or "leave it," with the right tone should be enough to achieve the desired shift in our dog's behavior.

We can learn to guide our dogs to be more emotionally dynamic and therefore more emotionally stable, which will allow them to be wild and free when it is appropriate, and calm and obedient when necessary. Having this balanced relationship will create a dynamic dog capable of thriving in all of life's uncertain situations.

The key distinction between a one-dimensional dog and a dynamic dog is in their psychological characteristics.

One-dimensional dogs tend to be psychologically fragile and erratic, while dynamic dogs are emotionally resilient and flexible. One-dimensional dogs tend to be at ease only when conditions permit. They may be relaxed and calm at home when everyone is there and nothing is going on, but the appearance of a passerby through the window sets them off. Within their routine, they may seem stable, but go on a road trip, put them in a crate, or take them on a coffee date, and they completely break down. The opposite is true for the dynamic dog; they can adapt to the situation presented and remain emotionally stable.

Lala, who for me epitomizes the dynamic dog, can remain calm and focused even in chaotic and disruptive environments, but can also go crazy and be wild at the park or in nature when I allow it. She adapts to the energy around her appropriately so that we can venture so much further together. In the chaotic energy of a public park on a Sunday, she can play and romp freely, but in the tranquil stillness of a library, she can be settled and serene. She can even stay absolutely calm in the Jiu-Jitsu gym among the intense energy of people sparring around her. People often comment on how stoic and relaxed she is in public. Even though she doesn't always gauge the situation perfectly on her own (it took time for her to acclimate to the Jiu-Jitsu gym and skate park), with my guidance, she is always as well-behaved as I need her to be. Because of the training we have done, she can flourish under almost any circumstance, which minimizes unnecessary stress for both of us. With her robust mind, she remains unflinching amid constant change in the world around her, creating a far superior quality of life for both her and me.

## Personal Growth

When we resign ourselves to taking a back seat in our dogs' personal growth and tolerate behavioral issues that indicate emotional instability, we are doing our dogs, ourselves, and our communities a disservice. While it takes work and effort to move through training successfully, it is arguably one of the most rewarding and fulfilling experiences we can have. Let's work toward building stronger, more substantial relationships with our dogs, thus strengthening their ability to live happily with us. By switching our perspective, we can recognize what we may have previously overlooked as opportunities to train our dogs and help them overcome their instinctual impulses. We can seek out distractions and gradually push our dogs out of their comfort zones until much of the world around them becomes familiar, which helps them grow into being dynamic and adaptable.

Helping many dogs and people grow, as well as working on my own personal growth, has shown me how fragile we can all be. Many of us have become one-dimensional. We have become so caught up in our likes and dislikes, our hopes and fears, our desires and aversions, that we have incapacitated ourselves in the face of a mysteriously unfathomable reality. Without becoming more dynamic ourselves, we will continually suffer throughout our lives.

A one-dimensional human is dependent on things going their way and matching their fixed beliefs to achieve happiness. In contrast, a dynamic human can find peace within any circumstance, no matter how undesirable or confounding. If we look closer, we find that even if we continue to exert the same amount of mental effort and continue buying into our sensitive inner monologue, the universe will continue to be an uncertain, seemingly hostile place with occasional miracles that surprise us. In his book *The Untethered Soul*, Michael Singer describes our excessive inner sensitivity as parallel to having thorns stuck in our bodies that we constantly try to avoid snagging on the world around us. He goes in-depth, explaining the choice to either avoid experiencing life deeply by preserving our inner sensitivities (the thorns), or to remove the root of these sensitivities, thereby enabling us the freedom to enjoy all aspects of our lives.

> "There's no reason to spend your life protecting the thorn [our sensitivities] from getting touched when you can just remove it. Once the thorn is removed, you are truly free from it. The same is true with your inner thorns; they can be removed. But if you choose to keep them without being disturbed by them, you must modify your life to avoid the situations that would stir them up. If you're lonely, you must avoid going to places where couples tend to be. If you're afraid of rejection, you must avoid getting too close to people."[24]

Instead of putting all this effort into trying to change the world around us, we could turn that energy inward. The practice of meditation is the practice of learning to come to peace with and thus removing all of our inner thorns: our fears, anxieties, and insecurities.

As Mark Manson describes it: "Meditation is, at its core, a practice of antifragility: training your mind to observe and sustain the never-ending ebb and flow of pain and not to let the 'self' get sucked away by its riptide."[25] In essence, meditation is training the mind to become dynamic, to become adaptable to the entirety of our life experience without the limitations of our narrow, projected preferences that try to pin down the mysteries of our universe.

## Paradoxes in Training

In life, we constantly face paradoxes that defy reason yet hold the most profound truths. In spiritual practice, as well as in training our beloved four-legged friends, these dualistic contradictions seem to be inescapable.

There is an ancient Sufi proverb that I love: "Trust in God, but tie your camel."

This idea epitomizes these paradoxes. In modern terms, I've translated it to: Have faith in yourself, your community, and the universe, but still lock your car. Or better yet: Live life freely, but train your dog. As human beings, we live between two realms—*being*, in which everything is perfect as it is, and *human*, in which we must traverse social arenas and competing agendas that can often feel hostile.

Human beings are inherently multidimensional.

When we get too involved in one of these realms and lose touch with the other, we begin to stray from a balanced and dynamic path. Without our ego, time, and logic, we will have a difficult time sustaining the body.

In our daily lives, we must exist in the realm of humanity to get to work on time, earn a living wage for the necessities of the body, and understand the social hierarchies that create the society we rely on to survive. Paying taxes, remembering Social Security numbers, phone numbers, and birthdays are all part of participating in our community. It is essential to use the mind to construct a life that can sustain us and our families, thereby fully embodying our humanness.

Without tending to the realm of being, of the soul, life becomes stale and unbearable, stripped of the mystery and wonder that give it depth—things like watching a sunset, feeling a breeze, or listening to music. When we lose the dynamic balance between the earthly and the spiritual, we risk the essence of our lives. This balance gives our lives depth and meaning. Therapist and author Thomas Moore shares the value of mysticality in *The Re-Enchantment of Everyday Life*: "Enchantment is the spell that spirits us away from familiar reality defined in one-dimensional terms."[26] When we live exclusively in the world of pragmatism, we fail to feed and nurture the soul, which causes deep internal suffering.

An authentically spiritual attitude bows to the soul, acknowledging it as an integral part of our everyday life. For when we honor our hearts, we can find a deep sense of purpose and significance within ordinary experiences—traffic jams, arguments with our partners, and clipping our toenails. These acts are no more or less spiritual than lighting incense for meditation, kneeling for prayer, congregating with a spiritual community, or any other practice or ritual. Gary Snyder addresses the spiritual depth of ordinary experience in his book *Practice of the Wild*: "Changing the filter, wiping noses, going to meetings, picking up around the house, washing dishes, checking the dipstick—don't let yourself think these are distracting you from your more serious pursuits. Such a round of chores is not a set of difficulties we hope to escape from so that we may do our 'practice' which will put us on a 'path'—it *is* our path."[27]

Our role as human beings is to merge the two domains, becoming dynamic in our expressions of life. We learn to see the pragmatism in meditation and the spirituality in ordinary activities. Again, Thomas Moore speaks to this multidimensional approach to living. He says, "When we have a radio playing as we work, we are straddling the literal realm of life and the enchanted world of art. We are doing what is most pleasing and necessary: living in the two realms at once."[28] In one plane, we are human—the organism, the animal, the body, the ego. In another, we are being—the soul, the atman, the brahman, the inner realm of dreams, thoughts, and emotions. To live fully is to hold both together, not as one, not as two, but as an ongoing paradox.

In working with ourselves or our dogs, we work within the realm of practicality to achieve a desired result, while honoring and accepting the perfection of the present moment exactly as it is. We can see this conundrum in how we work with our dogs. Shunryu Suzuki Roshi, in his masterpiece *Zen Mind, Beginner's Mind,* says of our essence: "You're perfect the way you are… and you could use a little improvement."[29]

There is no point where training will end—when our dogs will be perfect—and yet we strive to reach this point. There isn't always an inherent need to change our dogs' behavior, but we still work with them, growing the ever-deepening bond between us. Likewise, even though our growth will never end in reaching some apex of perfect character, we strive for that goal without aim, and all the while, we accept that we are perfect exactly as we are. Confused yet? Me too! Yet something about it, laughably, makes complete sense. These paradoxes riddle my line of work.

I get paid to see the best in dogs, and at the same time, improve them. If they are one with the universe and a perfect expression of themselves, then why do they need training? Why would we try to change something that is already perfect?

The universal process is ceaseless, constantly shifting and changing. Our genuine effort to become our ideal selves and develop the best versions of our dogs is a part of this process. The perfection of the universe, the Tao, lies within this impermanence. Suffering is part of the perfection and not separate from the experience of wholeness. Even our resistance to our suffering, our cravings and aversions, our kleshas, are part of it. Learning to accept and embrace the difficulties as a part of the path of life allows us to be at one with the present moment, to see the completeness in this step of our journey, at this point of the universe's unfolding.

Perfection is ungraspable.

The intellectual mind may create a concept of perfection, but it is nowhere close to encompassing the actual totality of the universe and the perfection within it. We cannot understand the greater scheme of things with our small, narrow, conditioned minds. Even the most enlightened human must think with a human brain. Even the most well-trained dog will still carry its animalistic instincts.

Though perfection is ungraspable, we can come to accept it.

By learning to withhold judgment, we can see every experience with openness as an opportunity to grow and appreciate all the colors of life. We don't have to fall victim to our own narrowness that wishes to put all of life into a comprehensible box. We can still have our preferences, while not letting them govern our ability to accept and welcome the present moment. We can create space in our lives to accept inevitable suffering, to appreciate even the challenging experiences that don't fit into our preconceived framework of reality. After all, these experiences are as much a part of life as any other, whether or not we understand them. Since they exist, we can at least learn to embrace them.

Withholding judgment is much easier said than done. It takes time and effort, but truly, there is no other path. Whether we realize it or not, we're either growing or remaining stagnant. As Viktor Frankl wrote, true freedom "is not freedom from conditions, but it is freedom to take a stand toward the conditions."[30] Real freedom is the ability to say "yes" to whatever life has to offer.

The practice of living dynamically applies to both ourselves and our dogs. Training is not about perfection—neither for our dogs nor for us—but about growth and adaptability within the ever-changing moment. We can honor the perfection that exists even amid imperfection. For true fulfillment, we can take responsibility for our growth and begin to become the people our dogs think we are, the people who our dogs truly deserve, while living full, dynamic lives together.

## CHAPTER 16

# Seeing the Bigger Picture

While working with our dogs, it's easy to get caught up in the current stage of the training and forget that it is one step in a long journey. In training your dog, there will be highs and, inevitably, lows. If you are struggling with something, you can become discouraged and frustrated. On the other hand, if your dog behaves particularly well, you may feel elated and proud. When our attention focuses narrowly on the current fleeting state, we fail to see the bigger picture, lacking the understanding that it is simply the next step on a greater path. Getting caught in this narrowness can lead to suffering for our dogs and ourselves.

## Broadening Our Perspective

In our everyday life with dogs, we often find ourselves in the trap of a limited perspective. At home, cuddling on the couch, we see our dogs as perfect angels that can do no wrong, but when that same pup is lunging at the end of the leash toward a squirrel or another dog, we paint the opposite picture in our mind's eye. A breakthrough in one area of training on one day does not mean that we will never experience difficulty in that area again. Similarly, a challenging moment does not take away from the progress we have made along the way.

We compartmentalize and deceive ourselves, seeing only what we wish to see and pushing everything else under the rug.

Dogs are not one way or the other.

Dogs are dogs and are inclined to behave in many different ways, depending on the conditions in which they exist, including how we handle them. Therefore, it's essential to fully appreciate that our dogs have the potential to be the pure beings we see in them, while also, if handled improperly, to be little monsters, causing harm and suffering. These are not mutually exclusive. Reality allows both to exist together.

The key may lie in our ability to see our dogs without judgment, a momentary lapse in our egoic projection. Even if your dog bites the delivery person, annoys you to hell with incessant barking, or chews up your brand-new shoes, you can still see the perfection that exists within their being. Even with all the behavioral issues, annoyances, and dysfunction, we can still love our dogs for who they are.

Our dogs do indeed have the purity we project onto them, but at the same time, they also have all the propensity of their animalistic instincts and devious inclinations. It is not either/or, but both. That is the distinction between our anthropomorphisms and reality. The former addresses what we wish to see, leaving out what doesn't match our beliefs; the latter encompasses exactly what is in front of us, allowing it to exist without projected judgment and resistance.

In seeing reality, we can refrain from reacting out of frustration during unwanted incidents, refrain from holding grudges when our dog's behavior shatters our idealistic expectations, and maintain structure consistently, even when our dogs behave well. All these moments are opportunities to learn and grow. This perspective leads to a much more balanced and healthy relationship with our dogs.

While our view of our dogs may not have total clarity, it lacks much of the judgment, doubt, and confusion of our relationship with ourselves and other humans in our lives. Even though we can accept and love our dogs for who they are, we can still see aspects of their character that need work. We can also easily recognize this same dynamic in our own lives. I often see myself and those around me going to similar extremes in relation to our life experiences. When the external conditions of life are favorable, we become ecstatic and joyful. Then, when our afflictions and unwanted behavioral tendencies confront us, we become anxious and depressed, and even feel self-loathing. When our pendulum swings back and forth drastically, we lose touch with the ground of reality, and these waves of emotion sweep us away.

## The Fleeting Nature of Emotions

A narrow perspective becomes excessive attachment to fleeting feelings.

Without recognizing the bigger picture, we can get lost in bouts of depression when we feel lonely or unfulfilled. We create identities out of our feelings. Instead of "feeling depressed," we identify with "being depressed." We feel that we *are* the depression and it consumes us. Thus, we have created a mental, conceptual identity out of a temporary, fleeting feeling. In doing so, we perpetuate the feeling each time we think, "I'm depressed," or "I'm lonely," or any other combination of negative emotions. In time, the sheer quantity of these feelings that continue to return overwhelms us, and we fear them every time. We anticipate and resist them.

When we resist these emotions, we add layers of fear and anxiety onto feelings that are already complex. We try to run from these emotions by distracting ourselves with excessive activity, fearing that a moment alone with ourselves may allow these unwanted feelings and associated thoughts to return. Instead of accepting and embracing the fleeting feeling of the moment and letting it go, we become stuck in a perpetual cycle of negative thinking and emotion. This identity attachment leads to deep, compounding suffering—what Buddhism calls *aversion*.

We also do the same thing with positive emotions. We feel on top of the world when we finally get that promotion, go on that first date, or buy that new gadget. But if we attach to these experiences or believe that's how we *should* feel all the time, our emotional state becomes dependent on circumstances that constantly shift and change. As the high from positive circumstances fades, as it inevitably will, we experience a void or feeling of incompleteness. We forget the impermanence of all feelings and grasp at our positive experiences. When we cling to our positive emotions and resist their unavoidable passing, it is called *craving*. A common example is the hangover after a fun night of partying. When we get caught up in the excitement of the party—consuming more than we probably should—we make shortsighted decisions that leave us sleep-deprived, dehydrated, and physically overwhelmed as we try to squeeze every last drop of enjoyment from the night. We sacrifice our well-being for fleeting moments of fun.

We can still enjoy life, but we can find peace and joy by embracing each moment, even when it seems inconsequential to the rational mind. When the present moment is no longer a means to an end, no longer a placeholder for some fantastical future, we can then appreciate and be grateful for each moment of our short lives that we get to spend on this earth.

The difference between boredom and relaxation lies only in our resistance.

Oftentimes when I feel bored or restless, inner resistance propels me to anxiously pace to figure out what would be the "best way" to spend my time. My mind races through various options, such as training my dog, working out, updating my social media accounts, catching up on emails, brainstorming projects, or editing my book. With so many things to do, decision fatigue and anxiety leave me exhausted. I could spend this time meditating and resting my body and mind, taking advantage of and relaxing into the lull in my busy life. However, my mind prioritizes efficiency, rendering these activities (or inactivities) unproductive. The irony is that in these moments, rest is what I need most and is the most productive thing I could be doing.

The idea of life without constantly anticipating—or grasping at—the next positive experience can seem bleak at first. Then what is there to look forward to? This question points directly at the problem of how we fundamentally approach life. By always needing something to "look forward to," we are, by definition, putting happiness out of reach in a mind-projected future. From here, we are left forever unsatisfied with the experience we are having *right now.*

So how can we approach life in a way that can bring more balance into our lives?

Buddhist literature expresses this idea as "the middle way." Walpola Rāhula, author of *What the Buddha Taught*, addresses the middle way "[a]s neither pessimistic nor optimistic. If anything at all, it is realistic, for it takes a realistic view of life and the world. It looks at things objectively. It does not falsely lull you into living in a fool's paradise, nor does it frighten and agonize you with all kinds of imaginary fears and sins. It tells you exactly and objectively what you are and what the world around you is."[31] Becoming attached to specific emotional states and the conditions that create them makes us discontented and unfulfilled. We cannot have an entire lifetime of positive experiences and avoid all negative experiences, although it seems our culture gravitates toward this belief. Accepting this reality takes the pressure off ourselves to set up the perfect algorithm of activity in our lives. It allows us to relax into our experience, without feeling the need to control everything. We can then interact with the world around us appropriately, withholding judgment born from irrational attachment to our fears and desires.

Recognizing the fleeting nature of emotion helps us to see the bigger picture and create a healthier relationship with our experiences, our emotional states, and our dogs. We can embrace both sides of the same coin and welcome either as they come, unaccompanied by the urge to control external circumstances that are beyond us. It takes consistent practice to retrain our conditioned minds that react with craving and aversion. We can maintain our composure and stay grounded during all of our experiences without losing ourselves in them. We see how much we have and, at the same time, see what we lack. We develop gratitude for our situation while learning to accept our pain. From this state, we find a deeper appreciation for the present moment and the profound connection we share with our dogs—one that reminds us to see the bigger picture and teaches us how to live fully and harmoniously in every circumstance.

## CHAPTER 17

# Wrapping Up

We often think of dog training as a means of teaching our dogs, yet through the training process, we can also learn a great deal from them. With the proper perspective, we can see that dogs have so much to teach *us* not only about how we interact with them, but also about our own experiences. This book brings together what I've learned about dogs through my work and life, and the lessons they have taught me in return. I hope that through my insights, you have learned as much about yourself as you did about your dog. For our dogs to transform their behavior, we must take the plunge first. From here, training dogs becomes a pathway for us to understand ourselves.

Training our dogs means committing to them and also to ourselves.

When we fully embody training as a lifestyle rather than an isolated activity, we can truly live the good life. Training should accompany us wherever we go, beyond formal training sessions. With consistent reinforcement of training techniques throughout the day, our dogs develop a deeper trust in our ability to make decisions for the pack. By limiting our dogs' unnecessary decision-making, we create space to prove to our dogs that we can lead effectively as we meet all our dogs' needs every day.

Furthermore, we also alleviate any stress involved with making authoritative decisions for the pack. As we consistently produce desirable outcomes with our decision-making, our dogs learn to look to our judgment in situations to which they would have previously reacted inappropriately. This shift occurs most dramatically when we adopt training as a way of life, incorporating it into all the areas where we find ourselves with our dogs.

The key to a healthier, deeper, and more balanced relationship with our dogs is a solid foundation of consistent structure, which allows us to set clear boundaries and build a deeper level of trust and respect between us. Most of all, it enables us to be far more consistent than we ever could be without it. Structure also provides guidance when we navigate unfamiliar or uncertain territory. Using tools such as the crate and techniques like the down-stay and the heel position, we can turn training into a lifestyle. Understanding our role in any situation allows us to communicate far more effectively, both inside and outside the home, than training without structure ever could.

Giving our dogs the freedom to make endless mistakes and then trying to hold them accountable leaves us exhausted. Since we will always play catch-up with this approach, training can seem a daunting and overwhelming chore. We can, instead, take it one step at a time, staying disciplined whether we feel inspired or not. Structure clearly shows our dogs exactly what we expect and holds them accountable to these expectations. From here, we can be much more supportive and engaged with the process of building a life with our dogs.

We don't train our dogs so we can have the best-trained dogs.

We train our dogs to cultivate a deeper and more meaningful relationship with the companions we share our lives with, while also growing into the best versions of ourselves.

Similar to dog training, our path can often seem an insurmountable journey. Within our busy lives, it may seem nearly impossible to fit in time for personal growth practices, such as meditation sessions, yoga, journaling, exercise, or reading. As life in society becomes more complex with technology, we find ourselves busier and busier with ever more responsibilities. Finding time to meditate may feel unattainable and even unproductive. With so much to do, why would we sit and do nothing? But without taking the time to sit with ourselves and our emotions, we will never truly know ourselves. We can structure our own down-stay time to develop our self-awareness. Without self-knowledge, we lack the awareness to recognize areas for growth, understand how our emotional baggage might be holding us back, or identify where we may be causing suffering for ourselves or our dogs. We can work smarter, not harder, with ourselves too, using tools to help us build healthy habits, cultivate a resolve to show up for ourselves, and trust in our ability to grow and transform.

We practice compassion and forgiveness when the conditions of life are favorable to prepare ourselves for the difficult times that inevitably come with the human experience. This practice deeply connects us with all sentient beings, for we all suffer and we all wish to be happy. Each of us will experience loss and hardship in our lifetimes, which will create pain. For me, the most significant motivating factor to develop a spiritual practice was to prepare for the eventual and inevitable loss of my dogs. I practice gratitude for the beautiful moments we spend together every day that I could so easily take for granted. I practice being present so I can feel fulfilled in my relationship, knowing that I was truly there to experience such a unique bond—there will never be another just like it. Honoring our special relationship has become the foundation for my life's journey. We can spend time practicing to understand ourselves and our habitual emotional reactions, which will help us bear the pain we inevitably experience in our lifetime. With healthy methods of processing and dealing with our pain, we can learn to feel it without prolonging it, identifying with it, or compounding it into deeper cycles of suffering. We can learn to heal and grow from our grief and hardship.

Without creating space to prioritize our mental and emotional health, we cannot perform at our best each day. As a dog trainer working alongside these deeply emotional beings, I must maintain a balanced mental and emotional state by being consistent with my daily practices.

In my experience, there is a direct correlation between my consistency with meditation practices, my stress levels, and the overall peace within a home that, at times, includes as many as ten or even twenty dogs. If I fail to do my practices consistently, I become less emotionally stable and more stressed. That energy then affects all the dogs, who start misbehaving and becoming restless. When I am consistent with my practices, I am calmer overall, which allows for more appropriate responses to the dogs' needs and a general tranquility among the pack.

To prioritize mental and emotional health, I highly recommend creating a schedule (structure!), whether it's a general morning or evening routine, specific events in your calendar, or setting alarms throughout the day. We can even choose a mundane, regular occurrence to help bring us back to the present. For instance, during my early days of training dogs, I had to drive all around Los Angeles every day, often getting stuck in traffic. One way I brought my practice along with me was to stop and follow my breath at every red light. Each time I hit a red light, even if I was late, which would usually induce a stress response or a feeling of impatience, it returned me to the present and face-to-face with my habitual behavioral reactions. Being able to hold ourselves accountable to something tangible helps create consistency and results. The time in our lives won't magically appear, but we can shift things around to reflect our deeper values, prioritizing our mental and emotional health—the same way we make time to train and spend time with our dogs.

We could watch thirty minutes less of television, cut down on our social media scrolling, or even dedicate time on our morning commutes to meditate, self-reflect, and be mindful. Once you have developed habits, frequently meditating, doing breathwork, yoga, or journaling can feel natural, productive, and easy. With habits built around our mental health, we can develop the same conviction in our self-growth that we have for our dogs' well-being.

By reflecting on how mental and emotional health and stability affect every aspect of our lives and follow us everywhere, we can see it as a high priority. Nothing affects your quality of life more than your mental and emotional health and stability. This insight can help us solidify our practices into daily habits that take precedence over the little escapes, such as our phones, TVs, or video games. Even though these options may be more entertaining, these small escapes from our emotional experiences will not create a more stable and peaceful life in or around us.

Without a firm intention, the distractions that surround us in daily life will easily sweep us away from our opportunities to grow. We may cut short our meditation or decide to forgo the discomfort of a workout that we told ourselves we would do. Rather than selling ourselves short, we can commit to our growth and a higher quality of life for ourselves and all those around us, including our dogs.

Learning to exercise our compassion, patience, joy, or forgiveness at work, at the gym, or in traffic can be a powerful tool of transformation. We can transform a traffic jam from a miserably frustrating inconvenience into a moment of connection to the suffering of everyone stuck on the road with us. We can turn our jealousy of a coworker's promotion into compassion for ourselves. We can transmute the uncertainty of the direction of our lives into celebrating the mysterious nature of our existence. The anger about our dog's misbehavior can be a wake-up call to the relationship we may have been neglecting. When we shift the way we relate to the world around us, life begins to open up to us, and every moment becomes an opportunity to grow.

We don't meditate to become the best meditator.

We meditate to ease the suffering for ourselves and those around us a little bit every day. We do it for our community, to build healthier and stronger relationships. We do it for all beings, seeing the interconnectedness of every being on this earth. We do it for ourselves to be the best selves we can be. And finally—though certainly not least—we meditate for our dogs. Because they deserve our highest selves, every day. From here, we can be the leaders that our dogs need us to be. We can approach training, for our dogs or ourselves, as a way of life to reduce the suffering and create more love and compassion in the world around us.

# About the Author

Adam Halleck is a professional dog trainer and Zen practitioner passionate about uncovering the wisdom in the ancient bond between dogs and humans. He uses a therapeutic and systematic approach to explore how we relate to our dogs—and ourselves. His approach blends the practical foundations of dog training with the insight and clarity of Zen, emphasizing  the subtle, emotional nature of the relationship—beyond technique. Through his transformational work, Adam invites readers to set aside their intellectual understanding of dog training and make space for something entirely new to emerge in their lives with their dogs.

To Adam, training dogs is a meditation, and when we're ready to learn, our dogs can show us the way. His dog, Lala, has been his most profound teacher, a true shepherd in every sense. Adam now lives with his partner and five dogs in Los Angeles, doing what he loves: helping dogs and people reach their fullest potential.

# Bibliography

1   Morell, Virginia. "How Wolf Became Dog." *Scientific American,* July 1, 2015. https://www.scientificamerican.com/article/ how-wolf-became-dog.

2   Dr. L. David Mech. "'Alpha' Wolf?" February 15, 2008. YouTube Video, 2:34. https://www.youtube.com/watch?v=tNtFgdwTsbJ.

3   Watts, Alan. *The Meaning of Happiness: The Quest for Freedom of the Spirit in Modern Psychology and the Wisdom of the East.* Harper & Brothers, 1940.

4   Ibid.

5   Kornfield, Jack. *A Path with Heart: A Guide Through the Perils and Promises of Spiritual Life.* Bantam, 1993.

6   Coyote, Peter. *Zen in the Vernacular: Things As It Is.* Inner Traditions/ Bear, 2024.

7   *Tom Davis Dog Training* and *No Bad Dogs Podcast:* "Brother Christopher of the Monks of New Skete." May 13, 2018. YouTube Video, 55:52. [14:23] https://www.youtube.com/watch?v=ZzF54yFd2lw.

8   Thich Nhat Hanh. *Being Peace.* Parallax Press, 2024.

9   Frankl, Viktor Emil. *Man's Search for Meaning: An Introduction to Logotherapy.* Beacon Press, 1992.

10  Tolle, Eckhart. *The Power of Now: A Guide to Spiritual Enlightenment.* Namaste Pub., 2004.

11  Thich Nhat Hanh. *The Art of Power: A Zen Master's Guide to Redefining Power, Achieving True Freedom and Discovering Lasting Happiness in a Stressful World.* HarperOne, 2007.

12  Magid, Barry. *Nothing is Hidden: The Psychology of Zen Koans.* Wisdom Publications, 2013.

13  Ibid.

14  Thich Nhat Hanh. *Being Peace.* Parallax Press, 2024.

15  Epstein, Mark. *Open to Desire: Embracing a Lust for Life – Insights From Buddhism and Psychotherapy.* Gotham Books, 2005.

16  Ibid.

17  Watts, Alan. *Tao: The Watercourse Way.* Souvenir Press Limited, 2019.

18  Watts, Alan. *Psychotherapy East and West.* New World Library, 2017.

19  Rinpoche, Yongey Mingyur, and Helen Tworkov. *In Love with the World: A Monk's Journey Through the Bardos of Living and Dying.* Random House Publishing Group, 2019.

20  Darwin, Charles. *The Expression of the Emotions in Man and Animals.* HarperCollins, 1999.

21  Horowitz, Alexandra. *Inside of a Dog: What Dogs See, Smell, and Know.* Simon & Schuster, 2010.

22  Ibid.

23  *Charlie Rose.* "Remembering Mr. Rogers (1994/1997)." February 27, 2016. YouTube Video, 15:18. https://www.youtube.com/watch?v=djoyd46TVVc.

24  Singer, Michael A. *The Untethered Soul: The Journey Beyond Yourself.* New Harbinger Publications, 2007.

25  Manson, Mark. *Everything Is F*cked.* HarperCollins Publishers, 2020.

26  Moore, Thomas. *The Re-Enchantment of Everyday Life.* Harper Perennial, 1997.

27  Snyder, Gary. *The Practice of the Wild.* North Point Press, 1990.

28  Moore, Thomas. *The Re-Enchantment of Everyday Life.* Harper Perennial, 1997.

29  Roshi, Shunryu Suzuki. *Zen Mind, Beginner's Mind: Informal Talks on Zen Meditation and Practice.* Shambhala, 2011.

30  Frankl, Viktor Emil. *Man's Search for Meaning: An Introduction to Logotherapy.* Beacon Press, 1992.

31  Rāhula, Walpola. *What the Buddha Taught.* Grove Press, 1974.